CALIFORNIA Science

Interactive Text

Macmillan McGraw-Hill

Contents

CHAPTER 1

Structure of Living Things

Vocabulary

 **cell** the smallest part of a living thing that can carry out processes of life

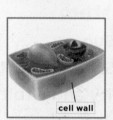 **vacuole** a cell part that holds food, water, and wastes

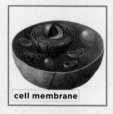 **cell membrane** a thin outer layer of a cell

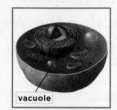 **cell wall** a hard outer layer of a plant cell that protects the cell and provides support

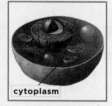 **cytoplasm** the gel-like material inside the cell that holds all the other inner parts of the cell

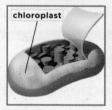 **chloroplast** a part of a plant cell that uses energy from sunlight to make food

 **nucleus** a large, round structure at the center of a cell that controls all the activities of a cell

 **organism** an individual living thing that can carry out all its own life activities

 **mitochondrion** the part of a cell that breaks down food and turns it into energy for the cell

 **tissue** a group of similar cells that do the same job in an organism

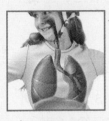 **organ** a body part made of different kinds of tissues that work together to do a certain job

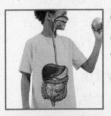 **organ system** a group of organs that work together to do a certain job

 **kingdom** the broadest group into which living things are classified

 **vertebrate** an animal that has a backbone

 **invertebrate** an animal that does not have a backbone

 **vascular** any plant that has tubes for moving water and other materials to where they are needed

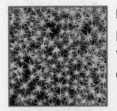 **nonvascular** any plant that soaks up water from the ground directly into its cells

 **fungus** an organism that cannot make its own food, but instead absorbs food from decaying organisms

 **bacteria** one-celled living things that do not have a nucleus

 **protist** a one- or many-celled organism that can either make, eat, or absorb food

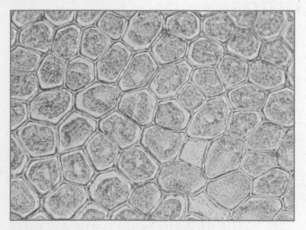

Plant cells often have boxlike shapes that fit closely together. This arrangement provides support for a plant.

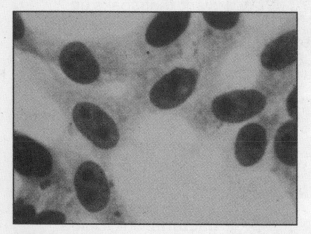

Animal cells have more rounded shapes than plant cells. Their shapes allow for movement.

What are plants and animals made of?

All living things are made of cells (SELZ). A **cell** is the smallest part of a living thing that can carry out life activities. That is, they take in food and grow.

Cells are the building blocks that all living things are made of. For example, your body is made of trillions of cells. A pet dog or cat is made of cells. A tree and even a blade of grass are made of cells.

There are different kinds of cells. Cells that make up plants are able to make food for a plant. They can store water. Cells that make up animals allow for taking in food, since animals do not make their own food.

✔ Quick Check

Fill in words to complete each sentence.

1. Living things _____ cells.

2. Plant cells _____ food.

How can cells be seen?

Cells are so small that you need a microscope (MIGH•kruh•skohp) to see them. A *microscope* makes things look bigger. Cells were first seen under a microscope over 400 years ago. It took almost 200 years of observing cells for scientists to understand that all living things are made of cells.

Microscope Timeline

1595—Zacharias Janssen creates the first compound microscope.

1670s—Dutch scientist Anton van Leeuwenhoek improves lens technology to magnify between 75 and 200 times.

1665—English scientist Robert Hooke studies slices of cork, calling the tiny boxes that he sees "cells" after a Latin word that means "little rooms."

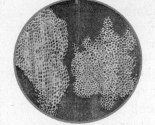

1860s–1890s— Scientists develop new ways of staining cells so they are easier to see and study under a microscope.

1940s—Electron microscopes magnify 40,000 times more than previous microscopes.

1600
1700
1800
1900

1982—Scientists build the scanning tunneling microscope that allows you to see individual blood cells.

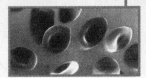

Reading Diagrams

Read the orange markers going from left to right on the timeline.

✔ Quick Check

List these people and discoveries in order from oldest to newest.

| electron microscope | Janssen | scanning tunneling microscope | Hooke |

3. oldest _____

_____ newest

What are the parts of cells?

Every cell has parts inside. Each part of a cell has a job that helps keep the cell alive.

Animal Cells

Look inside this animal cell. Find five parts in the cell. What job does each part have?

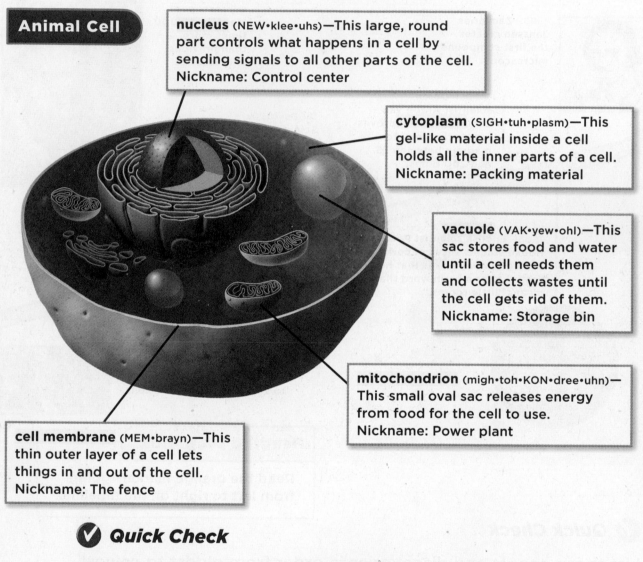

Animal Cell

nucleus (NEW•klee•uhs)—This large, round part controls what happens in a cell by sending signals to all other parts of the cell. Nickname: Control center

cytoplasm (SIGH•tuh•plasm)—This gel-like material inside a cell holds all the inner parts of a cell. Nickname: Packing material

vacuole (VAK•yew•ohl)—This sac stores food and water until a cell needs them and collects wastes until the cell gets rid of them. Nickname: Storage bin

mitochondrion (migh•toh•KON•dree•uhn)— This small oval sac releases energy from food for the cell to use. Nickname: Power plant

cell membrane (MEM•brayn)—This thin outer layer of a cell lets things in and out of the cell. Nickname: The fence

✔ Quick Check

Match the cell part with each statement.

4. ___ Stores food and water.   **a.** cell membrane

5. ___ Lets things in and out.   **b.** nucleus

6. ___ Controls cell activities   **c.** vacuole

Plant Cells

Plants cells have the same five parts that animal cells have. However, vacuoles in plant cells are a little different from the ones in animal cells. Also, plant cells have two additional parts.

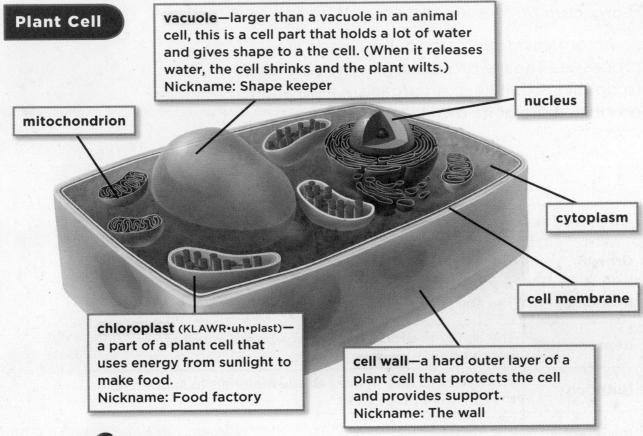

Plant Cell

vacuole—larger than a vacuole in an animal cell, this is a cell part that holds a lot of water and gives shape to a the cell. (When it releases water, the cell shrinks and the plant wilts.)
Nickname: Shape keeper

nucleus

mitochondrion

cytoplasm

cell membrane

chloroplast (KLAWR•uh•plast)— a part of a plant cell that uses energy from sunlight to make food.
Nickname: Food factory

cell wall—a hard outer layer of a plant cell that protects the cell and provides support.
Nickname: The wall

✔ Quick Check

Fill in the diagram with facts that explain the summary.

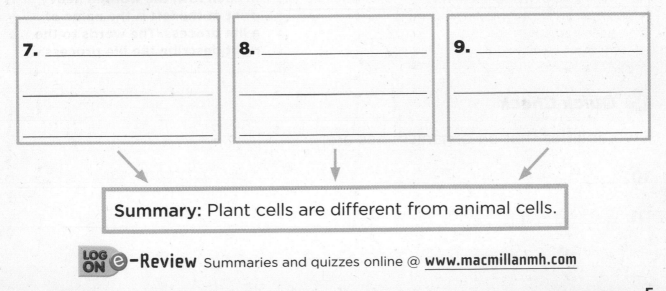

7. _____

8. _____

9. _____

Summary: Plant cells are different from animal cells.

LOG ON **e-Review** Summaries and quizzes online @ www.macmillanmh.com

How are living things organized?

The word we use for any individual living thing is **organism** (AWR•guh•nizm).

An organism can carry out the basic life processes. The *life processes* are the abilities to do things that keep an organism alive and to produce more of its own kind.

Life Processes in Living Things	
Growth	The ability to get bigger
Response	The ability to react to changes in the surroundings
Reproduction	The ability to produce offspring—that is, more of its own kind
Nutrition	The ability to take in food or raw materials to support the other life processes
Respiration	The ability to release energy from inside the food
Excretion	The ability to get rid of waste

Reading Charts

In each row, the word in heavy print at the left is the name of a life process. The words to the right describe the life process.

✔ Quick Check

Two abilities that an organism has are:

10. _____

11. _____

Kinds of Organisms

Remember, cells are the smallest part of a living thing. So, cells are the smallest part of an organism. Based on the number of cells, there are two kinds of organisms:

- **one-celled organisms** A one-celled organism carries out all its life processes in a single cell. One-celled organisms live in water, soil, and even on dust in the air.

- **many-celled organisms** People and all animals and plants are many-celled organisms. In a many-celled organism, each cell carries on life processes. However, the cells work together to do different jobs. For example, muscle cells in your heart work to keep your heart beating.

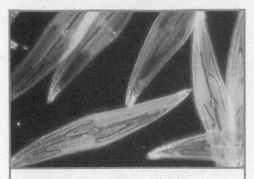

Diatoms are one-celled organisms. They are found in fresh water and salt water. You need a microscope to see them.

All plants and all animals, such as this mountain lion cub are many-celled organisms.

✔ Quick Check

How are one-celled and many-celled organisms alike and different?

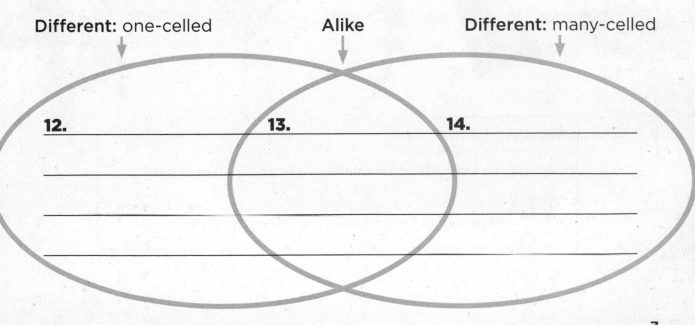

Different: one-celled   Alike   **Different:** many-celled

12. _____

13. _____

14. _____

How do cells work together?

Many celled organisms are made of different kinds of cells—such as blood cells, muscle cells, nerve cells, and so on. Each of these kinds of cells has a particular job.

Cells of the same kind work together doing their particular job. A group of the same kind of cells that do the same job is called a **tissue** (TISH•ew). Examples include:

- **animals** muscle tissue (which allows you to move), blood, nerves, bone, and skin
- **plants** tissue that carries water from roots to stems to leaves, flesh of fruits.

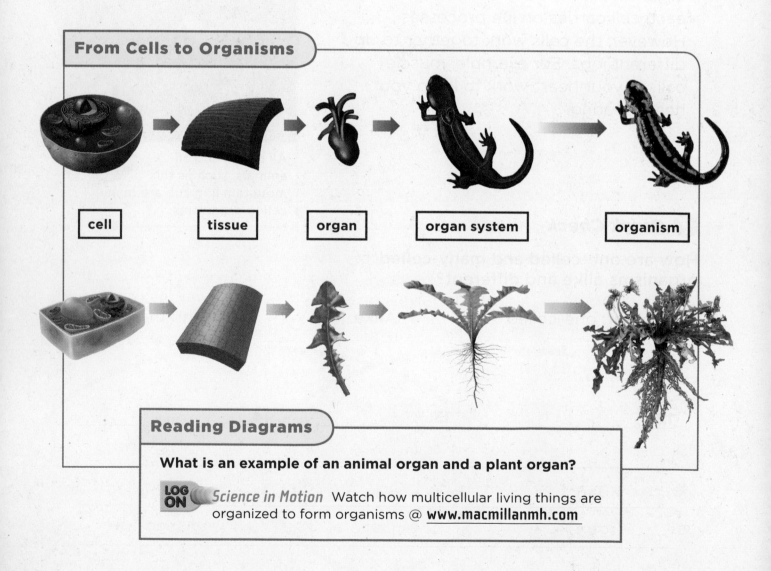

From Cells to Organisms

| cell | tissue | organ | organ system | organism |

Reading Diagrams

What is an example of an animal organ and a plant organ?

LOG ON *Science in Motion* Watch how multicellular living things are organized to form organisms @ www.macmillanmh.com

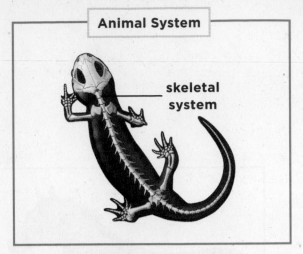

Animal System

skeletal system

The skeletal system is a support and movement system.

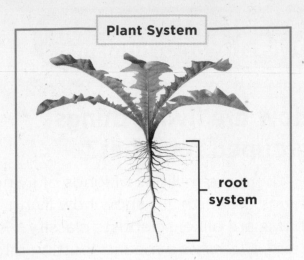

Plant System

root system

The root system is a transport system.

What are some plant and animal organ systems?

Tissues of different kinds come together to make up an **organ** (AWR•guhn). Examples are:

- **animals** brain, lungs, heart, stomach
- **plants** stems, fruits

A group of different organs that work together to do a certain job is an **organ system** (AWR•guhn). Examples are:

- **animals** system for breaking down food, transporting system, skeletal system
- **plants** root system, shoot system (stems and leaves)

✔ Quick Check

Write the letter of the meaning of each

15. ____ tissue

16. ____ organ

17. ____ organ system

a. a group of organs working together

b. many of the same cells working together

c. a group of tissues working together

LOG ON **e-Review** Summaries and quizzes online @ **www.macmillanmh.com**

How are living things grouped together?

There are millions of kinds of living things on Earth. To show how living things are alike, scientists classify them. *Classifying* means "putting into groups" based on how alike the living things are.

One way scientists classify living things is to put them into six kingdoms. A **kingdom** is the broadest group into which living things are classified.

Members of the same kingdom are then divided into smaller and smaller groups. The smaller the group, the more alike its members are.

The scientific name of a horse is *Equus caballus,* from its genus (*Equus*) and species (*caballus*).

- a kingdom is divided into phyla (*singular*, phylum).
- a phylum is divided into classes
- a class is divided into orders
- an order is divided into families
- a family is divided into genera (*singular*, genus)
- a genus is divided into species

✔ Quick Check

In each row, cross out one word that is out of order.

18. kingdom   phylum   order   class

19. order   family   species   genus

Classification of Horses

Start with the seven animals in the top row. As you go to each row below it, the one animal that is least like the others is removed.

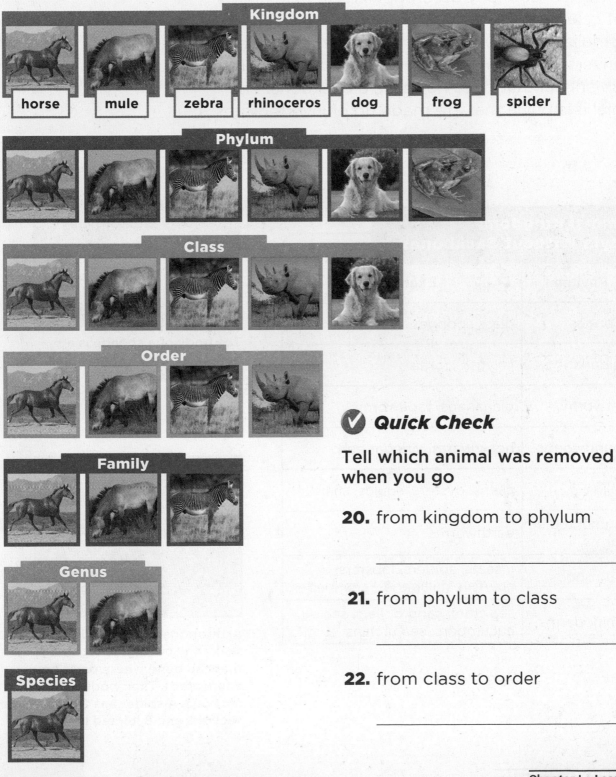

Kingdom
horse mule zebra rhinoceros dog frog spider

Phylum

Class

Order

Family

Genus

Species

✔ Quick Check

Tell which animal was removed when you go

20. from kingdom to phylum

_____

21. from phylum to class

_____

22. from class to order

_____

What do animals have in common?

All animals belong to one kingdom, the Animal Kingdom. How are all animals like?

- All animals are many-celled living things.
- All animals get energy from eating other living things.

There of so many different kinds of animals that scientists divide them into many phyla (that is, smaller groups). Many of the phyla are made up of invertebrates (in•VUR•tuh•brayts). An **invertebrate** is an animal that does not have a backbone. The table lists phyla that are made up of invertebrates.

The body of a sponge is a hollow tube with small holes. Sponges trap food that is carried into their bodies by water.

Animal Kingdom: Phyla Without Backbones

Phylum	Examples
Sponges	glass sponges
Cnidarians	jellyfish, corals
Flatworms	planarians, tapeworms
Roundworms	hook worm, vinegar eel
Mollusks	clams, oysters, squids, snails
Segmented worms	earthworms
Arthropods	insects, spiders, lobsters, crayfish, millipedes, centipedes
Echinoderms	sea stars, sand dollars, sea cucumbers, sea urchins

Arthropods have a hard outer skeleton and jointed legs (legs that can bend where parts are connected). Their bodies are in sections. A spider has 2 body sections and 8 jointed legs.

Phylum *Chordata*

Animals we are most familiar with—such as frogs, dogs, cats, and horses—belong to another phylum, *Chordata* (KAWR•day•ta). Members of this phylum have a supporting rod that runs the length of their body for at least part of their life.

This phylum includes some unusual water-dwellers such as sea squirts. Sea squirts are invertebrates. However, most members of this phylum are vertebrates (VUR•tuh•braytz). A **vertebrate** is an animal that has a backbone.

This phylum is divided into many classes. Here are the classes that are made up of vertebrates.

Animal Kingdom: Phylum Chordata Classes with Backbones	
Class	**Examples**
Jawless fish	lampreys
Cartilage fish	sharks, rays, skates
Bony fish	most familiar fish of sea and fresh water
Amphibians	frogs, salamanders, toads
Reptiles	snakes, lizards, turtles, alligators
Birds	ducks, chickens, robins, ostriches, penguins
Mammals	dogs, cats, squirrels, horses,tigers, lions, humans

Fish live in water. They have gills for taking in oxygen from water. Most familiar fish are bony fish— they have skeletons and jaws.

A cow is a mammal. Mammals have hair or fur and young are fed from their mother's milk.

✓ Quick Check

Cross out the animal that does not belong in each row.

23. frogs   birds   clams   fish   horses

24. sponges   earthworms   sea stars   spiders   sharks

What do plants have in common?

All plants are many celled living things. They can all produce their own food.

Most common plants are vascular (VAS•kyuh•luhr) plants. **Vascular** plants have tubes running up and down inside. The tubes bring water and minerals from the ground up to roots and stems into the leaves. They bring food from the leaves to other parts of the plant.

On the other hand, mosses are nonvascular (non•VAS•kyuh•luhr) plants. **Nonvascular** plants do not have tubes for moving water and other materials. They soak up water directly from the soil into their cells. To do so, they must grow very close to the ground.

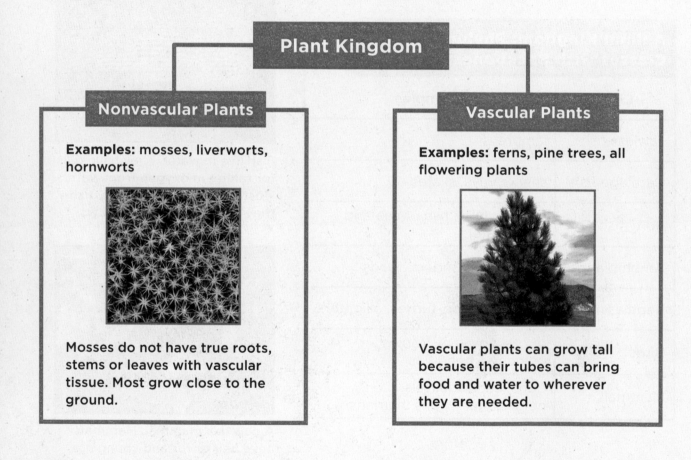

Plant Kingdom

Nonvascular Plants

Examples: mosses, liverworts, hornworts

Mosses do not have true roots, stems or leaves with vascular tissue. Most grow close to the ground.

Vascular Plants

Examples: ferns, pine trees, all flowering plants

Vascular plants can grow tall because their tubes can bring food and water to wherever they are needed.

✔ Quick Check

25. All plants are alike because they can _____.

26. Mosses are not like pine trees because mosses do not have

_____.

Structure of Living Things

What are fungi?

Mushrooms often grow from the ground. So people often mistake them for plants. However, a mushroom is not a plant. It is a fungus (FUNG•guhs). A **fungus** cannot make its own food, as plants can. A fungus absorbs food from dead organisms in their surroundings. Fungi (FUN•ji), which means more than one fungus, can be one celled or many celled. They can be helpful or harmful.

Helpful Fungi	Harmful Fungi
• Some break down dead organisms into materials that enrich soil	• Wild mushrooms can be poisonous.
• Yeasts can make bread rise.	• Some cause disease, such as athlete's foot.
• Some are used in medicines, such as this mold, which produces penicillin.	• Some attack crops, such as wheat rust and this corn smut.

✔ Quick Check

27. One way a fungus is different from a plant is that a fungus

_____.

What are bacteria?

Bacteria (bak•TEER•ee•uh) are one-celled living things. Remember that cells have a part called a nucleus, the cell control center. Bacteria do not have a nucleus. They do have other parts, such as a cell membrane and cytoplasm. Most have cell walls.

Bacteria make up two kingdoms. True bacteria may cause diseases. However, many are helpful such as bacteria in your digestive system that help you digest food. Bacteria are used to produce yogurt and other foods.

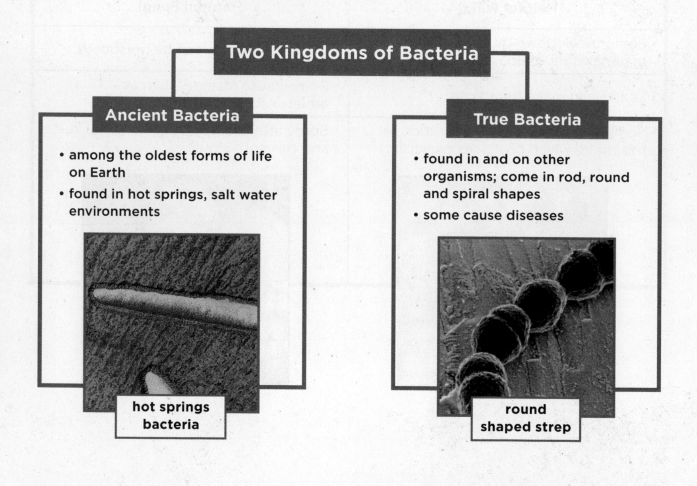

Two Kingdoms of Bacteria

Ancient Bacteria

- among the oldest forms of life on Earth
- found in hot springs, salt water environments

hot springs bacteria

True Bacteria

- found in and on other organisms; come in rod, round and spiral shapes
- some cause diseases

round shaped strep

✅ Quick Check

28. Bacteria are not like other cells because bacteria

_____

What are protists?

Protists (PRO•tists) are living things that do not fit any other kingdom. They may be one celled or many celled. Also:

• some make their own food, like plants
• some eat other living things, like animals
• some break down dead organisms, like fungi

However, they are much simpler than plants, animals, and fungi.

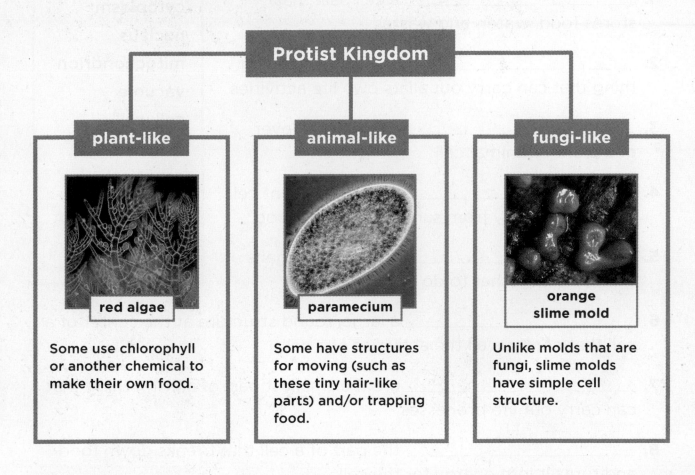

Protist Kingdom

plant-like

red algae

Some use chlorophyll or another chemical to make their own food.

animal-like

paramecium

Some have structures for moving (such as these tiny hair-like parts) and/or trapping food.

fungi-like

orange slime mold

Unlike molds that are fungi, slime molds have simple cell structure.

✔ Quick Check

List one thing that each protist can do

29. plant-like protists _____

30. animal-like protists _____

LOG ON e-Review Summaries and quizzes online @ www.macmillanmh.com

Structure of Living Things

Use a word from the box to name each example described below.

cell
cell membrane
cytoplasm
nucleus
mitochondrion
vacuole
cell wall
chloroplast
organism
tissue
organ
organ system

1. _____ a cell part that stores food, water, and wastes

2. _____ an individual living thing that can carry out all its own life activities

3. _____ a thin outer layer of a plant or animal cell

4. _____ a part of a plant cell that uses energy from sunlight to make food

5. _____ a group of organs that work together to do a certain job

6. _____ a large, round structure at the center of a cell that controls all the activities of a cell

7. _____ are the smallest part of a living thing that can carry out life processes

8. _____ the part of a cell that breaks down food and turns it into energy for the cell

9. _____ the gel-like material inside the cell

10. _____ a group of similar cells

11. _____ a body part made of different tissues

12. _____ a hard outer layer of a plant cell

Fill in the blanks. Then find the same words in the puzzle.

1. An organism that cannot make its own food, but instead

   absorbs food from decaying organisms _____

2. a one-celled or many-celled organism that can either make, eat,

   or absorb food _____

3. Any animal that has a backbone _____

4. The broadest group into which living things

   are classified _____

5. An animal that does not have a backbone _____

6. One-celled living things that do not have

   a nucleus _____

7. Any plant that has tubes for moving water and other

   materials to where they is needed _____

8. Any plant that soaks up water from the ground directly

   into its cells _____

```
T F N O N V A S C U L A R
F Y S Z X Y F Q A D M C I
K I N G D O M G J H O W C
W N A V V A S C U L A R V
Q C B A E L M W R O S X J
A X Q B R B L M W E E S N
Z D J W T W H F D U T D M
Q V Q S E Q O G H P G U H
N U Q Q B A C T E R I A R
I N V E R T E B R A T E W
W B U S A W T S I T O R P
F G X A T S S U G N U F W
H U K X E R E N O A R G U
```

Clue: #1 and #2 are backwards.

CHAPTER 2

Plant Structures and Functions

Vocabulary

spore a single cell that can develop into a new plant exactly like the plant that produced it

seed

seed an undeveloped plant with stored food inside a protective coat

angiosperm a seed plant that produces flowers

gymnosperm a seed plant that does not produce flowers

pollination the movement of pollen to the seed-making part of a flower

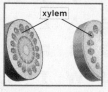

xylem

xylem tissue that moves water and minerals up from the roots

How do plants produce, transport, and use food?

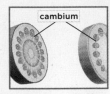

phloem tissue that moves food (sugar) from the leaves to other parts of a plant

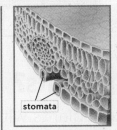

stomata tiny holes in the bottom of a leaf that allow gases in and out

cambium a layer of cells that makes xylem and phloem

respiration (in cells) the release of energy from food

photosynthesis how a plant changes raw materials into food in the presence of sunlight

Vascular Plants

seedless plants

fern

horsetail

What are vascular plants?

Trees, bushes, grass, and plants with vegetables or fruits are all vascular plants. A vascular plant has special tissues that form thin tubes inside the plant. These tubes carry water and other materials up and down the plant.

These tubes connect the three main parts of a vascular plant:

roots Roots have several jobs:
• anchor plants to the ground
• take in water and minerals from the soil
• store food made by the plant (in some plants)

stems Stems have several jobs:
• support the plant above ground
• move materials from the roots to the leaves and from the leaves to the roots

leaves Leaves have one main job:
• make food for the plant

(which have roots, stems, and leaves)

seed plants

no flower

flowers

evergreen

cycad

flowering plant

gerbera daisy

Classifying Vascular Plants

There are two ways vascular plants reproduce, that is, form offspring (more of their own kind).

seedless plants Plants such as ferns do not have seeds. They grow from spores (spawrz). A **spore** is a single cell that can develop into a new plant. The new plant is exactly like the plant that produced the spore.

seed plants Most familiar vascular plants make and grow from seeds. A **seed** contains an undeveloped plant and stored food inside a protective coat. Some seed plants produce flowers. Some do not.

✔ Quick Check

Match each word with its description.

1. _b_ root   **a.** undeveloped plant with food and a coat

2. _c_ leaf   **b.** part that takes in water and minerals

3. _d_ spore   **c.** part that makes food for a plant

4. _a_ seed   **d.** single cell that develops into a plant

How are seedless and seed plants different?

Mosses, ferns, and horsetails are seedless plants. They grow from spores. Here is an example.

- On a fern, spores are found in spore cases on the underside of a fern leaf (a frond).
- When a spore case opens, many spores come out. Some fall to the ground. Some are carried by wind.
- Spores grow into new ferns, just like the parent fern, if they land in moist soil.

Grasses, trees, and flowering plants are seed plants.

- Seed plants produce two special kinds of cells: *male cells* and *female cells*.
- A seed forms when a male cell and a female cell join together into one cell.
- Inside a seed there is a new, undeveloped plant, as well as food. The new plant shares characteristics of the two cells that joined when the seed was made.

Spores and Seeds

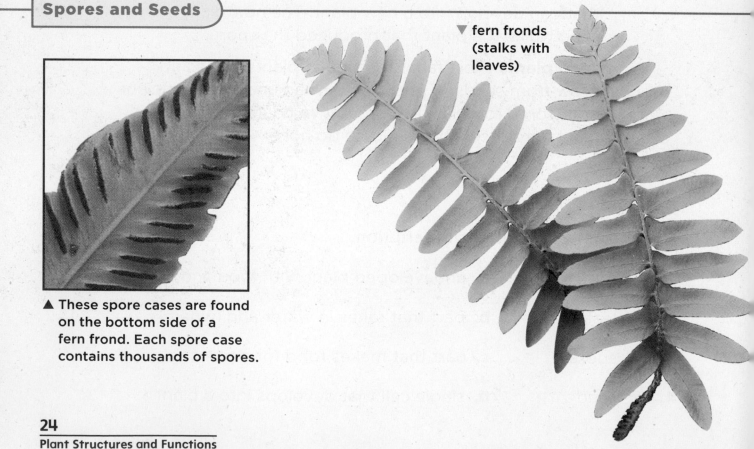

▲ These spore cases are found on the bottom side of a fern frond. Each spore case contains thousands of spores.

▼ fern fronds (stalks with leaves)

Classifying Seed Plants

Most seed plants produce flowers. Some do not.

Seed plants that produce flowers are called **angiosperms** (AN•jee•uh•spurmz). There are over 235,000 kinds of angiosperms, from rose plants to orange trees.

Seed plants that do not produce flowers are called **gymnosperms** (JIM•nuh•spurmz). Gymnosperms produce seeds inside a cone. When the cone falls, the seeds are released.

Evergreens are gymnosperms. These trees lose their leaves slowly all year. When a leaf is lost, a new one grows back. So, these trees look green all year.

✔ **Quick Check**

Fill in the diagram to show how you can classify vascular plants and then seed plants.

First Start with all vascular plants.

⬇

5. Next Classify vascular plants into _SEED_ and _SEEDLESS_.

⬇

6. Last Classify seed plants into _FLOWERING_ (ANGIOSPERMS) and _NON-FLOWERING_ (GYMNOSPERMS).

▼ Apples are fruits that contain seeds. The seeds can be planted to grow new apple trees.

◀ apple tree branch

Reading Photos

You can get an up-close look at spores and seeds by looking at the picture in each red box.

What do flowers do?

When you think of flowers, you may think of bright colors and sweet scents. Flowering plants use their flowers for reproduction, that is, making new plants. The diagram shows the parts of a flower:

- **stamen** The stamen (STAY•men) is the male part of a flower. It produces male cells called pollen grains.
- **pistil** The pistil (PIS•tuhl) is the female part of a flower. It produces female cells called egg cells.
- **ovary** The ovary (OH•vuh•ree) is the bottom part of the pistil. Egg cells are found in the ovary.

Seeds will form in the ovary. To learn how, follow the steps on the next page.

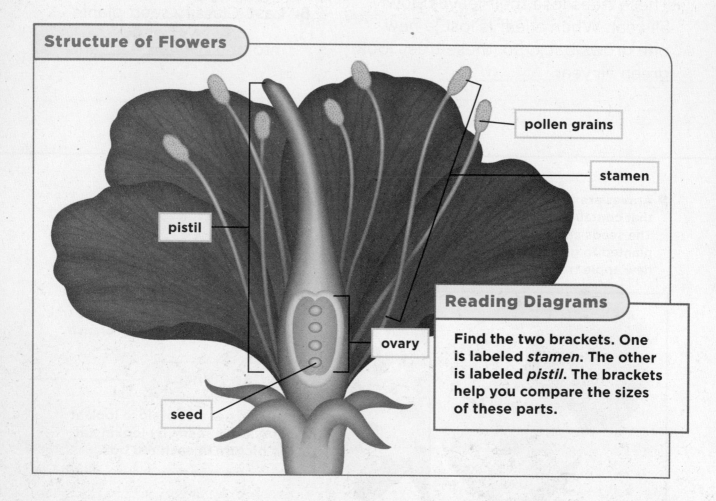

Structure of Flowers

pollen grains

stamen

pistil

ovary

seed

Reading Diagrams

Find the two brackets. One is labeled *stamen*. The other is labeled *pistil*. The brackets help you compare the sizes of these parts.

Seeds

Look back at the diagram as you follow the steps.

1. **pollination** Pollen grains collect on the top of a stamen. They are moved to the pistil of the same flower or another flower. **Pollination** (pol•uh•NAY•shuhn) is the movement of pollen grains from a stamen to a pistil. What moves the pollen grains?
   - *wind*
   - *insects and birds* are attracted to flowers by the colors and smells. They brush up against the stamens and pick up the pollen grains on their bodies. They drop the grains onto other flowers.

2. **making a seed** When a pollen grain reaches a pistil, it travels down into the ovary. A pollen and an egg cell can then join and form a seed. The ovary slowly enlarges, becoming a fruit with the seeds inside.

3. **scattering seeds** Seeds are then scattered by wind or animals.

   If a seed reaches a place where the soil is moist and the temperature is just right, the new plant inside begins to grow.

✔ Quick Check

Summarize the story of a seed.

7. First _Pollination occurs_

8. Next _Pollen & egg form seed_

9. Last _Seeds are scattered_

LOG ON ℮-Review Summaries and quizzes online @ www.macmillanmh.com

How do different materials move in plants?

A tree may look still. However, materials are moving inside a tree. Vascular plants have tubes running through the roots, stems, and leaves. These tubes bring materials up to the leaves. The leaves make food (sugar). The sugar then is carried to the rest of the plant.

Transport in Vascular Plants

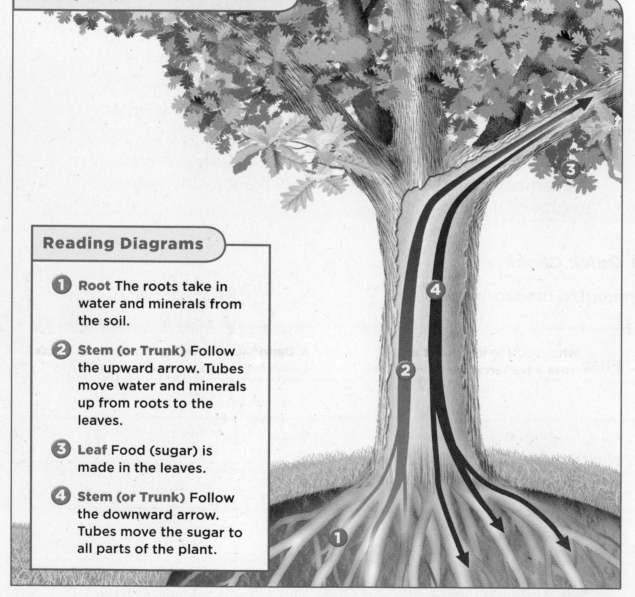

Reading Diagrams

1. **Root** The roots take in water and minerals from the soil.

2. **Stem (or Trunk)** Follow the upward arrow. Tubes move water and minerals up from roots to the leaves.

3. **Leaf** Food (sugar) is made in the leaves.

4. **Stem (or Trunk)** Follow the downward arrow. Tubes move the sugar to all parts of the plant.

Roots

Inside a root, are tiny tubes made of vascular tissue. Toward the center, **xylem** (ZIGH•luhm) moves water and minerals up from the ground through the root to the stem.

Around the center, **phloem** (FLO•em) carries sugar from the leaves down the stem and into the root.

Roots come in many sizes and shapes. Carrots and beets have thick *taproots* that grow deep into the soil. Grasses have thin, *fibrous* roots. Corn plants have finger-like *prop* roots.

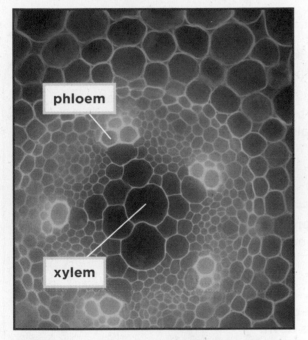

▲ This is what you see if you cut a thin slice across a buttercup root and look at it through a microscope.

▲ Dandelions have taproots. These roots can reach water deep in the ground.

✓ Quick Check

10. How does water from the ground get all the way up to a leaf?

Through Xylem in center of stem

11. Why are two kinds of tubes needed in a plant?

One to go up & one to go down

What is the transport system made of?

You saw that a root has two kinds of tubes made from vascular tissue, xylem and phloem. They continue up from the root all the way through the stem.

In different kinds of stems, the xylem and phloem are arranged differently. See the diagram. There is a layer of cells called cambium (KAM•be•uhm) in both stems. **Cambium** is where new cells of xylem and phloem are made.

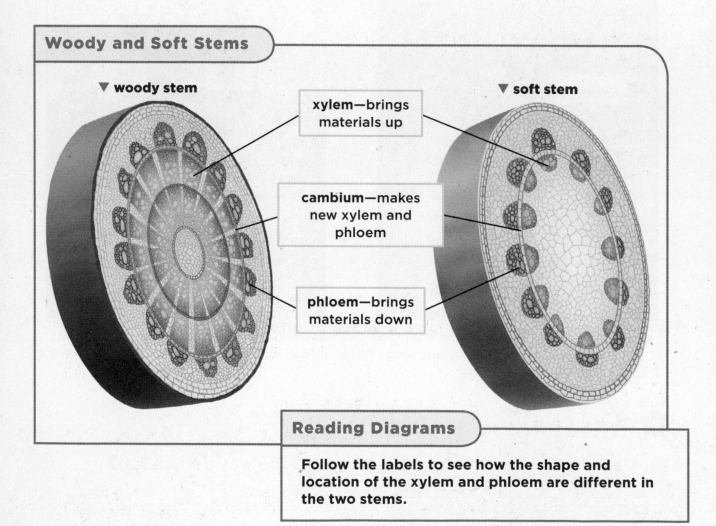

Woody and Soft Stems

▼ woody stem

▼ soft stem

xylem—brings materials up

cambium—makes new xylem and phloem

phloem—brings materials down

Reading Diagrams

Follow the labels to see how the shape and location of the xylem and phloem are different in the two stems.

Tree Rings

A tree stump gives you a view of the outside and inside of a woody stem, a tree trunk.

- **bark** Along the outside is a layer of bark. Bark protects the trunk.
- **phloem** Just inside the bark is a layer of phloem.
- **xylem** Inside the phloem are rings. The rings are layers of xylem.

A ring of xylem grows every year. So by counting the rings you can tell the age of the tree. Start from the inside, the oldest part. Each ring has two parts.

- **light part** The lighter part grows in the spring when water is usually plentiful.
- **dark part** The dark part grows in the fall when there is less rain.

Counting tree rings gives you the age of a tree. The oldest living tree is a bristlecone pine in California. It is 4,767 years old. ▼

✔ Quick Check

What happens in a stem? Give a cause or effect in each row.

Cause	→	Effect
Xylem dries up and dies.	→	**12.** _Becomes Heartwood_
13. _Phloem dries up_	→	Sugar cannot move down the stem.
14. _New Xylem Tissue forms_	→	A thick ring grows in the spring.

LOG ON **e-Review** Summaries and quizzes online @ **www.macmillanmh.com**

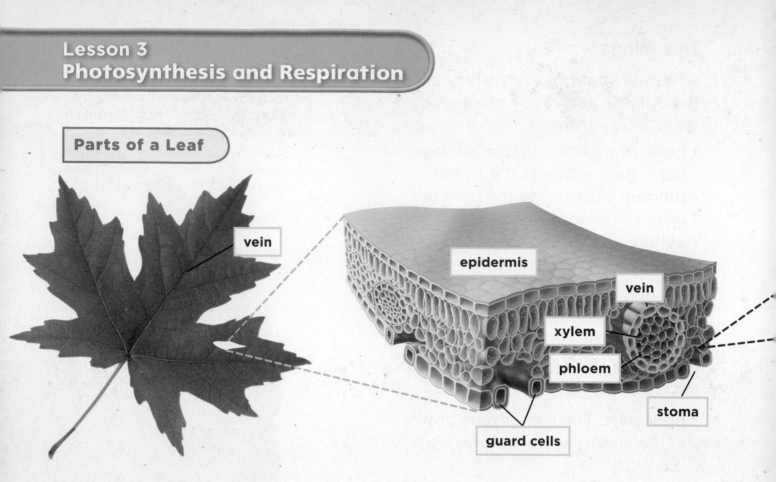

Parts of a Leaf

vein

epidermis

vein

xylem

phloem

stoma

guard cells

What do leaves do?

A leaf is a factory that makes food (sugar). To make food, a leaf needs two raw materials: water and carbon dioxide.

Look at the diagram to see how a leaf gets these two raw materials:

- **veins** A plant takes in water from the soil. The water travels up the xylem through the roots and the stem. The xylem goes into a leaf through narrow veins. Water enters the leaf through the xylem.

- **stomata** Stomata (STOH•muh•tuh) are tiny holes in the bottom of a leaf or stem. (The word for one hole is *stoma*.) The stomata are surrounded by guard cells. When the guard cells open the stomata, carbon dioxide comes in. Guard cells can close the stomata to keep a plant from drying up.

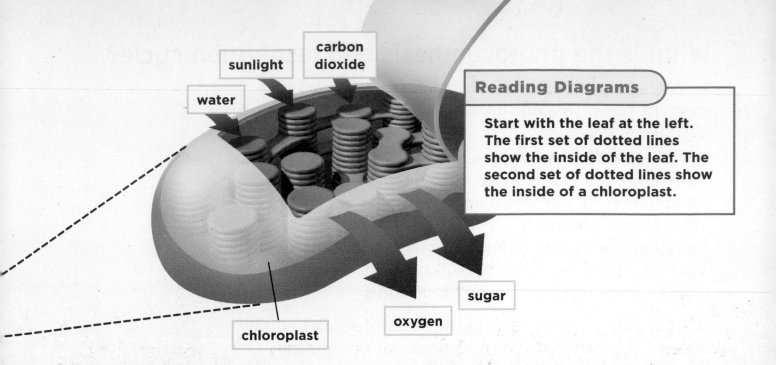

sunlight

carbon dioxide

water

Reading Diagrams

Start with the leaf at the left. The first set of dotted lines show the inside of the leaf. The second set of dotted lines show the inside of a chloroplast.

sugar

oxygen

chloroplast

Food Making

Here is an outline of the food-making process, **photosynthesis** (foh•tuh•SIN•thuh•sis),

- **where it happens** Food is made in cells just under the epidermis (ep•i•DUR•mis). The epidermis is the outermost layer of a leaf. (It is also made in cells of some stems.) Food is made in chloroplasts. Chloroplasts are cell parts with a green substance that traps sunlight.
- **what happens** Carbon dioxide and water enter the chloroplasts. In the presence of sunlight, these two raw materials combine. They form sugar and oxygen.

carbon dioxide + water + energy ⟶ sugar + oxygen

- **after it happens** Phloem carries the food to all parts of the plant. Oxygen goes out the stomata.

✔ Quick Check

Cross out the word that does not belong in each row

15. **Parts of a leaf:** vein   ~~root~~   epidermis

16. **Raw materials:** ~~sugar~~   water   carbon dioxide

17. **What a leaf makes:** ~~energy~~   oxygen   sugar

What is the photosynthesis and respiration cycle?

In photosynthesis, a plant makes food (sugar) and oxygen. These two products are used by the plant, and also by animals.

- **sugar (food)** The food has energy stored in it. Animals that eat plants take in the food with its stored energy. Other animals that eat plant-eaters also get the food and stored energy.
- **oxygen** Plants and animals use oxygen for the process of respiration (res•puh•RAY•shuhn) in cells. **Respiration** in cells is the release of energy from food.

Respiration takes place in the parts of a cell called mitochondria. Oxygen and sugar go into the mitochrondria. The oxygen breaks down the sugar and energy is given off. Two waste products are made in the process: carbon dioxide and water.

sugar + oxygen ⟶ carbon dioxide + water + energy

Respiration in a Cell

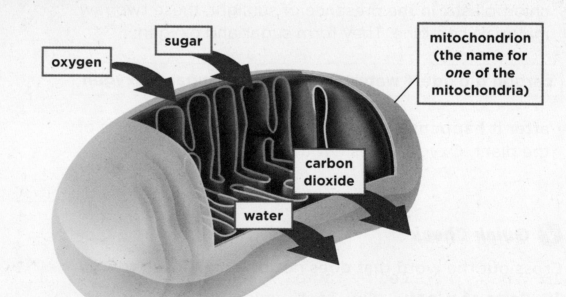

oxygen

sugar

mitochondrion (the name for *one* of the mitochondria)

carbon dioxide

water

Animals and plants give off the two waste products, carbon dioxide and water. Plants then take in carbon dioxide and water and use them to make food. The two processes, photosynthesis and respiration, happen over and over again.

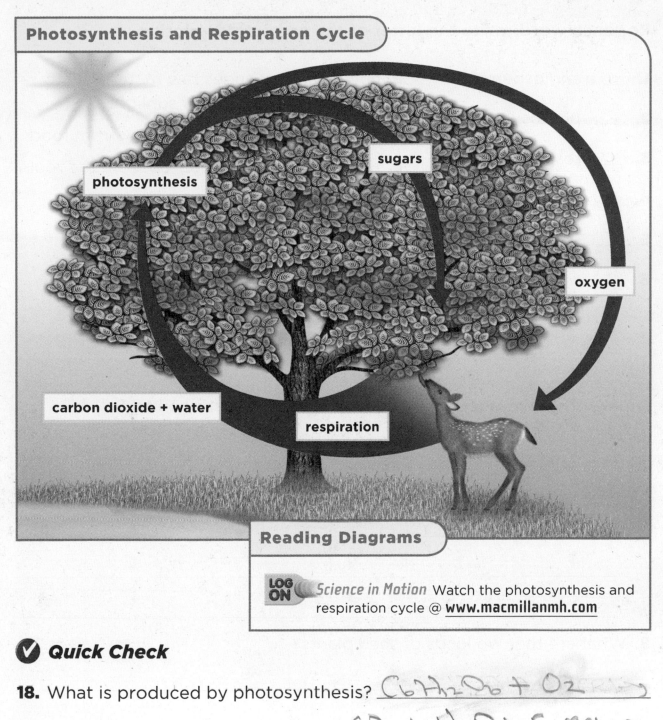

Photosynthesis and Respiration Cycle

sugars

photosynthesis

oxygen

carbon dioxide + water

respiration

Reading Diagrams

LOG ON *Science in Motion* Watch the photosynthesis and respiration cycle @ **www.macmillanmh.com**

✔ *Quick Check*

18. What is produced by photosynthesis? $C_6H_{12}O_6 + O_2$ energy

19. What is produced by respiration? $CO_2 + H_2O +$ energy

LOG ON **e-Review** Summaries and quizzes online @ **www.macmillanmh.com**

Plant Structures and Function

For each word, write the letter of the correct description.

1. _f_ angiosperm

2. _a_ photosynthesis

3. _b_ respiration

4. _d_ stomata

5. _e_ gymnosperm

6. _c_ xylem

a. how a plant changes raw materials into food in the presence of sunlight

b. (in cells) the release of energy from food

c. tissue that moves water up from the roots to the leaves

d. tiny holes in the bottom of a leaf that allows gases in and out

e. a seed plant that does not produce flowers

f. a seed plant that produces flowers

Answer the two questions. Use words from questions 1 to 6 in each answer.

7. What are two processes that happen over and over again? Explain your answer.

_____ photosynthes & respiration _____

_____

_____

8. What are the two kinds of seed plants?

_____ angiosperm & gymnosperm _____

_____

Fill the missing words in the blanks below. Then find and circle those words in the puzzle at the bottom of the page.

1. A single cell that can develop into a new plant exactly like

   the plant that produced it is called a(n) _____Spore_____.

2. An undeveloped plant with stored food inside a

   protective coat is a(n) _____seed_____.

3. Tissue that moves food (sugar) from the leaves to

   other parts of a plant is called _____phloem_____.

4. A layer of cells that makes xylem and phloem is called

   _____cambium ring_____.

5. The movement of pollen to the seed-making part of

   a flower is called _____pollination_____.

6. Tissue that moves water and minerals up from the roots

   _____xylem_____.

CHAPTER 3

Human Body Systems

Vocabulary

digestion breaking down food into simpler substances that your body can use

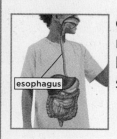

saliva a watery fluid that softens and moistens food

salivary glands

esophagus the long muscular tube that brings food into the stomach

esophagus

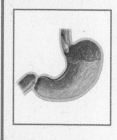

stomach a muscular organ that changes food into a thick soupy liquid

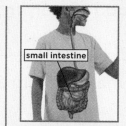

small intestine

small intestine the organ that completes digestion and allows digested food to enter the blood

large intestine the thick tube-like organ that removes undigested waste

diaphragm

diaphragm a large, flat muscle that pulls air in and pushes air out of the lungs

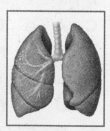

lung one of the two organs that fills with air when you inhale

How does your body work?

 **alveoli** air sacs in the lungs where gases move into and out of the blood

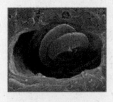 **capillary** a tiny blood vessel

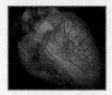 **heart** a muscular organ that constantly pumps blood throughout the body

 **artery** a thick-walled blood vessel that carries blood away from the heart

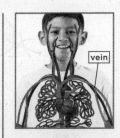 **vein** a blood vessel that carries blood back to the heart

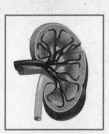 **kidney** an organ that filters certain body wastes out of the blood

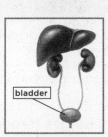 **bladder** an organ that stores liquid wastes from the kidneys temporarily

 **nephron** a part of the kidneys where waste materials are separated from useful materials in the blood

What are the organ systems in your body?

The human body is organized to do many jobs at the same time.

- The smallest part of the body is the cell, such as blood cells.
- Similar cells working together to do a job make up a tissue.

- Different tissues working at the same job make up an organ.
- Organs working together at certain jobs form an *organ system*.

Organ systems work together to carry out all your life activities.

Human Organ Systems

System	Summary
skeletal	made of 206 bones, which support and protect the body and give it shape
muscular	made of muscles, which move the skeleton and make up some organs
respiratory	brings oxygen to lungs and then to the body cells and gets rid of carbon dioxide
circulatory	uses the heart, blood, and blood vessels to move materials to and from cells
excretory	uses skin, lungs, and kidneys to remove wastes from the body
nervous	sends messages throughout the body by way of the brain, spinal cord, and nerves
digestive	uses the mouth, stomach, and small intestines to turn food into nutrients that the cells of the body can use
immune	protects and fights against disease and helps heal injuries
skin	protects the body from injury and germs and removes some wastes
endocrine	produces chemicals that travel in the blood to control growth and other activities
reproductive	produces offspring (that is, more of one's own kind)

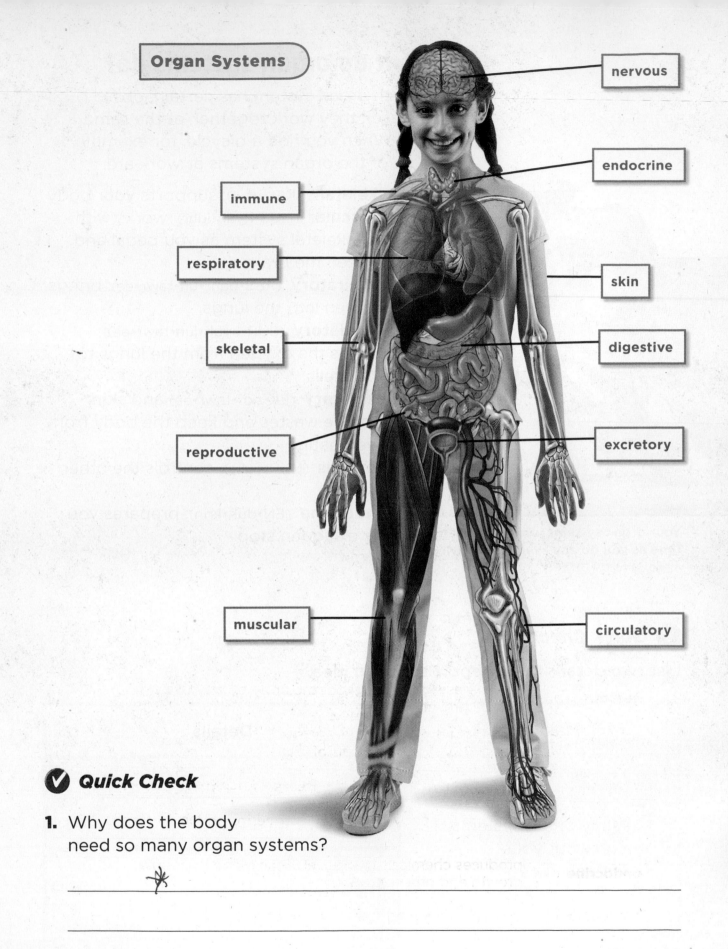

Organ Systems

nervous

endocrine

immune

respiratory

skin

skeletal

digestive

reproductive

excretory

muscular

circulatory

✅ *Quick Check*

1. Why does the body
   need so many organ systems?

_____

_____

What do organ systems do?

Each organ system has certain jobs. However, they work together, at the same time. When you ride a bicycle, for example, some of the organ systems at work are:

- **skeletal** (SKEL•i•tul): supports your body
- **muscular** (MUS•kyuh•luhr): works with the skeletal system as you pedal and tighten the brakes
- **respiratory** (RES•puhr•uh•tawr•ee): brings oxygen into the lungs
- **circulatory** (SUR•kyuh•luh•tawr•ee): carries the oxygen from the lungs to your cells
- **excretory** (EK•skri•tawr•ee) and **skin**: remove wastes and keep the body from overheating
- **nervous** (NUR•vuhs): controls the other systems
- **endocrine** (EN•duh•krin): prepares you for a sudden stop

Your organ systems work at the same time as you do any everyday activity.

✓ Quick Check

List two details that support the main idea.

Main Idea	Details
Many organ systems carry out your life activities.	2. Resp & Circulatory work together to carry oxygen to every cell 3. skeletal & muscular

How are body materials transported?

Materials are moving through your body all the time. They include nutrients from the foods you eat, oxygen that you inhale, and wastes from your cells. Four organ systems are working together to move these materials. These organ systems are your body's *transport systems*.

A highway is a transport system for cities.

Transport Systems of the Human Body

System	What It Transports	Summary
digestive	food and nutrients	moves food through digestive organs and breaks it down into nutrients
respiratory	oxygen	moves oxygen into lungs, where it is picked up by circulatory system
circulatory	nutrients, oxygen, wastes	carries oxygen and nutrients to cells, carries wastes away from cells
excretory	wastes such as carbon dioxide, sweat	uses blood to carry wastes to organs that remove them from the body

✔ Quick Check

4. How is a highway similar to transport systems of the body?

Highway transports people & goods like body systems transport stuff

5. Why is the excretory system important? Like GARBAGE Removal

LOG ON e-Review Summaries and quizzes online @ **www.macmillanmh.com**

What is digestion?

Every cell in your body needs energy to live and grow. This energy comes from food. However, food has to be broken down into a form your cells can use. Breaking down food into simpler substances that your body can use is called **digestion** (die•JES•chuhn).

Here is how food reaches your cells:

1. When you bite into and chew food:
   • your teeth and tongue break the food into small pieces
   • chemicals in your mouth break down some of the food into nutrients.

   A *nutrient* is a simple form of food that your cells can use.

2. The process continues in other organs where food is broken down further.

3. The nutrients eventually pass into your blood. Blood carries them to your cells. The nutrients give your cells energy and materials for growing.

Your digestive system starts working on food in your mouth.

✔ *Quick Check*

6. Why is digestion an important life process?

_____

_____

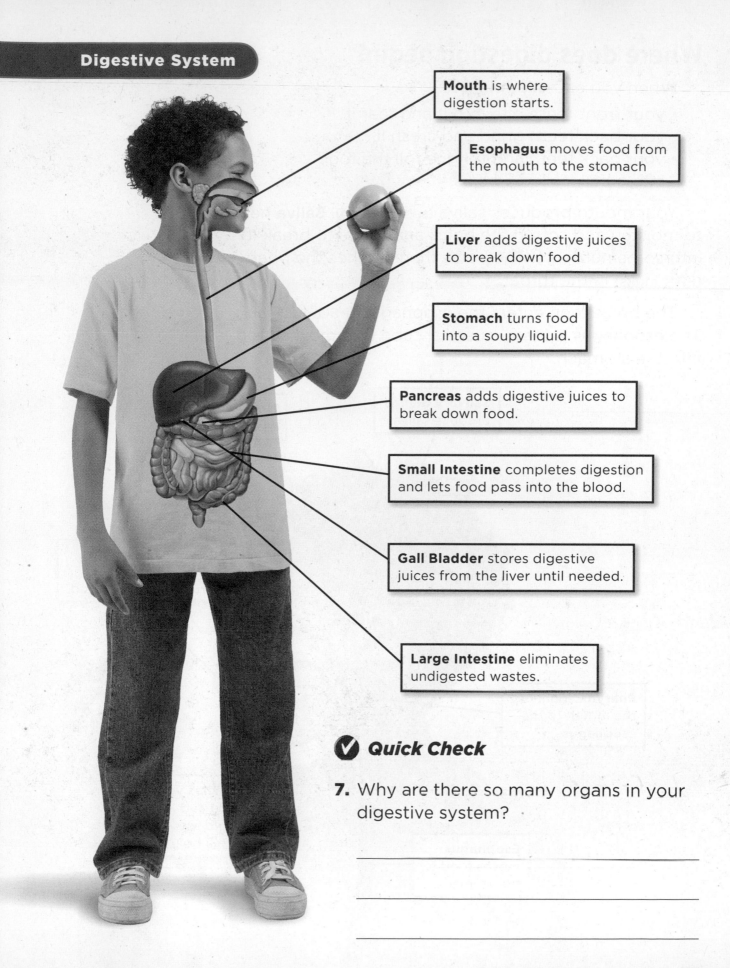

Mouth is where digestion starts.

Esophagus moves food from the mouth to the stomach

Liver adds digestive juices to break down food

Stomach turns food into a soupy liquid.

Pancreas adds digestive juices to break down food.

Small Intestine completes digestion and lets food pass into the blood.

Gall Bladder stores digestive juices from the liver until needed.

Large Intestine eliminates undigested wastes.

✔ Quick Check

7. Why are there so many organs in your digestive system?

_____

_____

_____

Where does digestion begin?

When you eat an apple

- your front teeth bite into it and tear it
- your back teeth grind and crush it
- your back teeth and tongue roll the food into a ball, called a *bolus*.

Your mouth produces saliva (seh•LIE•vuh). **Saliva** helps to moisten and soften the bolus and starts to break it into some nutrients. The bolus then reaches the pharynx (FAR•ingks) in the throat.

The bolus then enters the esophagus (i•SOF•uh•guhs). The **esophagus** is long, muscular tube that moves food into the stomach.

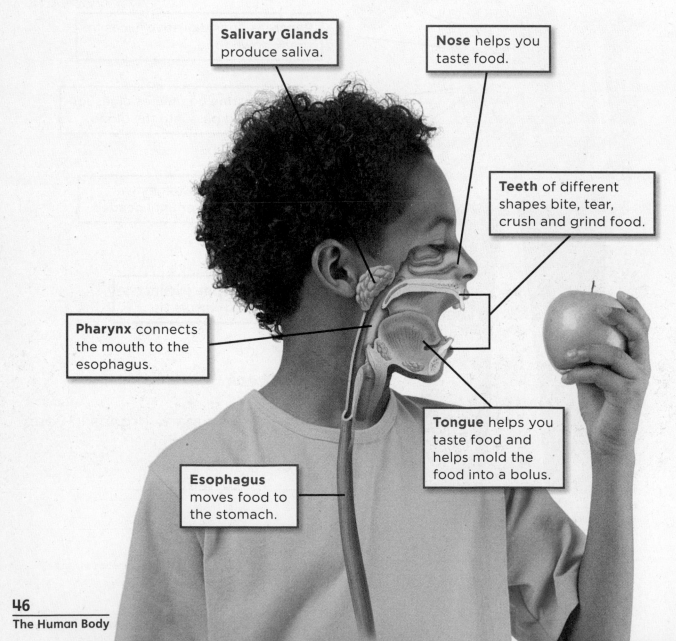

Salivary Glands produce saliva.

Nose helps you taste food.

Teeth of different shapes bite, tear, crush and grind food.

Pharynx connects the mouth to the esophagus.

Tongue helps you taste food and helps mold the food into a bolus.

Esophagus moves food to the stomach.

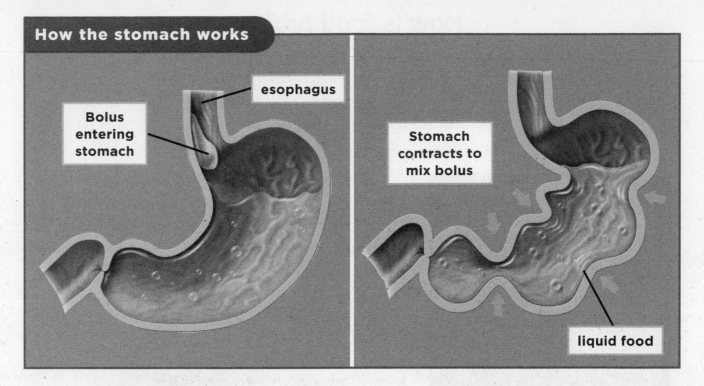

How the stomach works

Bolus entering stomach

esophagus

Stomach contracts to mix bolus

liquid food

The Stomach

The bolus enters the stomach. The **stomach** is a digestive organ with muscular walls.

- The walls of the stomach produce chemicals that break down the bolus further into nutrients.
- The muscles in the walls of the stomach squeeze (contract) and relax over and over. This muscle action mixes up the bolus with the chemicals.

After about 4 to 6 hours of squeezing and mixing, the bolus has become a thick, soupy liquid. The liquid then moves into the next digestive organ.

✓ Quick Check

Match each word with its description

8. ____ moves food into the stomach   **a.** stomach

9. ____ moistens the bolus in the mouth   **b.** teeth

10. ____ tears and crushes food   **c.** esophagus

11. ____ turns food into a soupy liquid   **d.** saliva

How is food broken down further?

When food leaves the stomach, it moves into an organ that has folds in its walls. That organ is the small intestine. The **small intestine** is a long, coiled tube-like organ. The folds are a clue to what happens there.

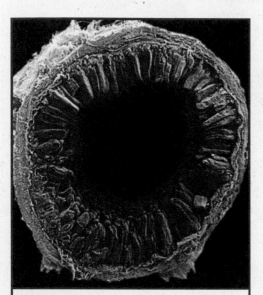

The fingerlike folds in the walls of the small intestine soak up nutrients.

Other parts of the digestive system pour digestive juices into the small intestine:

- the *pancreas* adds juices that digest most kinds of foods.
- the *liver* adds *bile*, which breaks up fats.

As food moves through the long small intestine:

1. the juices mix with food until it is all broken down into nutrients.

2. the folds in the walls of the small intestine soak up the nutrients.

3. In the folds, the nutrients pass into tiny blood vessels. Blood carries the nutrients to the cells.

✔ Quick Check

Fill in the diagram. Summarize digestion into three main steps.

12. First _____

↓

13. Next _____

↓

14. Last _____

What are the parts of the large intestine?

Not everything that you chew is digested. Undigested parts of the food are a form of waste. This waste moves from the small intestine into the large intestine. The **large intestine** is a thick tube-like organ that removes undigested waste from the body.

In this organ, wastes move through three parts:

• cecum (SEE•kuhm)
• colon (KOH•luhn)
• rectum (REK•tuhm)

Solid waste, *feces* (FEE•seez), is pushed out from the rectum. It leaves the body through the *anus* (AY•nuhs). This process is called elimination (i•li•muh•NAY•shuhn).

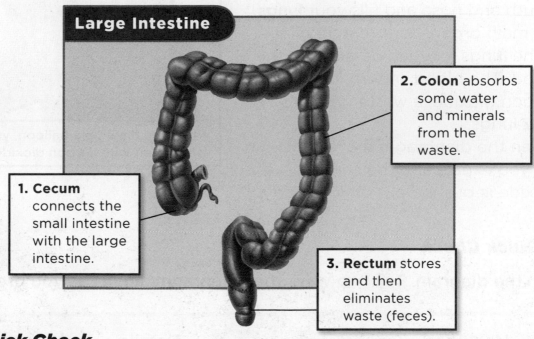

Large Intestine

2. Colon absorbs some water and minerals from the waste.

1. Cecum connects the small intestine with the large intestine.

3. Rectum stores and then eliminates waste (feces).

✔ *Quick Check*

15. How is the job of the large intestine different from the job of the small intestine? _____

_____

LOG ON ⓔ-**Review** Summaries and quizzes online @ www.macmillanmh.com

What does the respiratory system do?

You breathe all the time, even while you sleep. Breathing is a job of your respiratory system. This system works to take in oxygen from the air and bring it to your blood. Your blood brings oxygen to all your cells. Here's how it works:

- You have a muscle, the **diaphragm** (DIGH•uh•fram), that works to pull air in and push air out of your body,
- When the diaphragm pulls down, you inhale (in•HAYL). Air enters your mouth and nose and fills your **lungs**, the main organs for breathing.
- In the lungs, oxygen passes into the blood. The blood, in turn, drops off carbon dioxide, a waste gas, into your lungs.
- When the diaphragm moves back up, you exhale and the carbon dioxide is pushed out of your body.

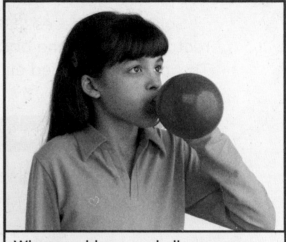

When you blow up a balloon, you are exhaling air with carbon dioxide.

✔ *Quick Check*

Fill in the diagram. Tell two ways the diaphragm moves as you breathe.

Main Idea	Details
The diagram controls your breathing.	**16.** inhale _____ _____ **17.** exhale _____ _____

Epiglottis This flap of tissue closes when you swallow and keeps food from entering the airway.

Nose You breathe (inhale and exhale) air through your nose.

Throat Air from your mouth passes down the pharynx and over the voice box (larynx).

Mouth Air from your nose enters your mouth. You can also breathe through your mouth.

Trachea Air passes into this strong tube, which divides into two branches.

Lungs You have two lungs. They fill with air when you inhale.

Bronchi These are the two branches of the trachea. Each leads into a lung and divides into smaller branches.

Diaphragm This flat sheet of muscle pulls air in and pushes air out of the lungs.

Alveoli These are small sacs at the end of each tiny branch of the bronchi. This is where oxygen reaches the bloodstream.

Quick Check

18. Put these words in order to show how oxygen gets into your blood.

mouth   trachea   alveoli   bronchi

Where does gas exchange take place?

As you inhale, air enters your nose and mouth. Air follows this path:

- Air moves through the trachea (TRAY•chee•uh), a thick tube that leads into smaller and smaller tubes, ending with the bronchi (BRONG•kigh).
- The bronchi lead to air sacs called **alveoli** (al•VEE•uh•ligh). The alveoli are surrounded by tiny blood vessels, **capillaries** (KAP•uh•ler•eehs).
- In the alveoli, oxygen from the air goes into the blood in the capillaries. Carbon dioxide leaves the blood and enters the alveoli. Carbon dioxide is exhaled.

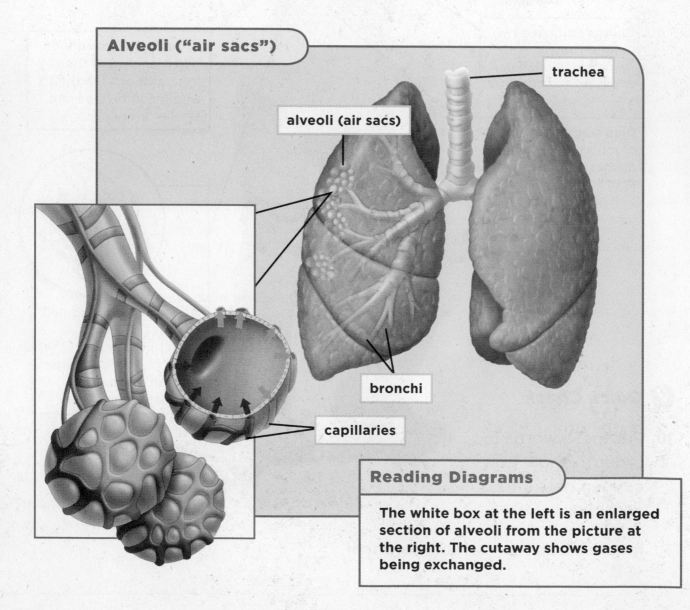

Alveoli ("air sacs")

trachea

alveoli (air sacs)

bronchi

capillaries

Reading Diagrams

The white box at the left is an enlarged section of alveoli from the picture at the right. The cutaway shows gases being exchanged.

How does respiration happen in animal cells?

What happens to oxygen in the blood? The oxygen is picked up by red blood cells. Blood is also carrying sugar from digested food.

When blood flows through a capillary, sugar and oxygen move into body cells. In a body cell, they go to the mitochondria. Here

respiration takes place. The oxygen is used to break down the sugar and release energy. Two wastes are produced, carbon dioxide and water. Blood cells carry carbon dioxide back to the lungs, where it is exhaled. You'll learn later how water is removed.

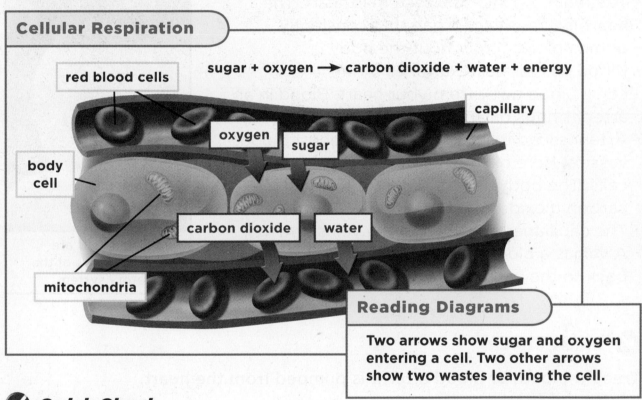

Cellular Respiration

sugar + oxygen → carbon dioxide + water + energy

red blood cells

capillary

oxygen

sugar

body cell

carbon dioxide

water

mitochondria

Reading Diagrams

Two arrows show sugar and oxygen entering a cell. Two other arrows show two wastes leaving the cell.

✔ Quick Check

19. Two gases exchanged in the air sacs are _____ and carbon dioxide.

20. Blood carries oxygen and _____ to body cells.

21. Body cells release carbon dioxide and _____.

How are materials transported through your body?

Your circulatory system is a "delivery system." Red blood cells travel in the blood, bringing things to and from your body cells.

- The main organ of the system is heart. The **heart** is a muscular organ that constantly pumps blood throughout the body.
- Blood vessels called **arteries** (AHR•teer•ees) carry blood away from your heart. Blood in an artery brings oxygen and food to body cells.
- Arteries lead to capillaries, the thinnest blood vessels. Here oxygen and food pass into body cells. The body cells release wastes, such as carbon dioxide, into the blood.
- The capillaries now lead to the veins (VAYNZ). A **vein** is a blood vessel that carries blood back to the heart.

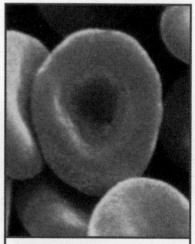

Red blood cells are the messengers of the circulatory system.

✔ Quick Check

Trace the path of blood after it is pumped from the heart.

22. First _____

↓

Next The vessels described above lead blood to capillaries.

↓

23. Last _____

Vein Veins carry blood back to the heart. The blue color is used to show blood with carbon dioxide.

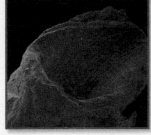

Artery Arteries carry blood away from the heart. The red color is used to show blood with oxygen.

Heart A heat beats 70 to 90 times a minute, pumping blood throughout your body.

Capillary This is the thinnest kind of blood vessel. Only one red blood cell at a time fits through.

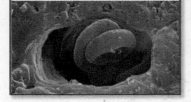

✅ *Quick Check*

24. Why is the heart the *main* organ of the circulatory system?

_____

25. Red is used to show blood that has _____.

How can systems work together?

The circulatory and respiratory systems work together. Here's how:

- Veins bring blood into an upper "chamber" of the heart called an *atrium* (AY•tree•uhm).
- From an atrium, blood flows through a *valve* to a lower "chamber," called a ventricle (VEN•tri•kul).
- Blood is pumped out of the ventricle through an artery.

The Heart

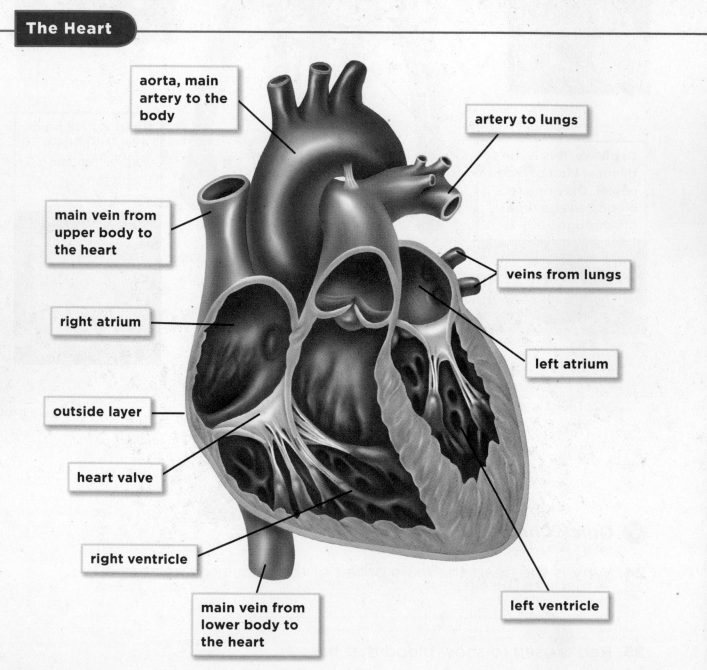

aorta, main artery to the body

artery to lungs

main vein from upper body to the heart

veins from lungs

right atrium

left atrium

outside layer

heart valve

right ventricle

left ventricle

main vein from lower body to the heart

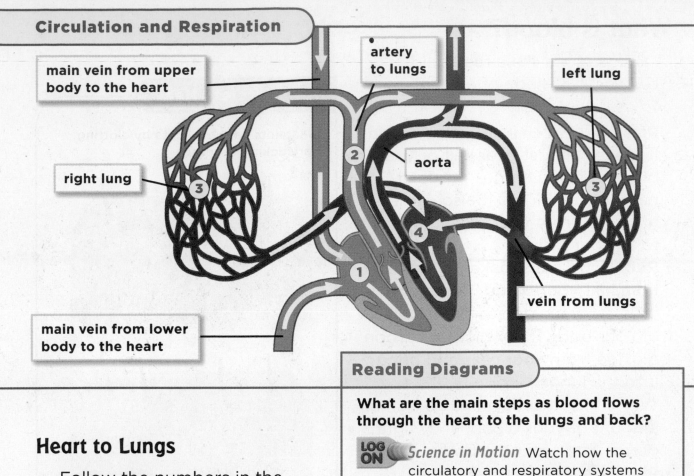

main vein from upper body to the heart

artery to lungs

left lung

right lung

aorta

main vein from lower body to the heart

vein from lungs

Reading Diagrams

What are the main steps as blood flows through the heart to the lungs and back?

LOG ON *Science in Motion* Watch how the circulatory and respiratory systems work together@ **www.macmillanmh.com**

Heart to Lungs

Follow the numbers in the diagram as you read.

1. Veins bring blood with carbon dioxide to the right side of the heart.

2. The blood is pumped through an artery to the lungs.

3. In the lungs, blood drops off carbon dioxide. Blood takes in oxygen.

4. Veins bring oxygen-rich blood to the left side of the heart. It is pumped out to the body through a main artery, called the *aorta* (ay•AWR•tuh).

✔ Quick Check

26. Why does the heart pump blood to the lungs?

_____

What is blood?

Blood looks like a red liquid. However, it is made of a liquid *and* cells.

- **Plasma** (PLAZ•muh) is a clear liquid. It makes up just over half of your blood. Plasma carries the solid parts of the blood. It also carries nutrients from your digested food to all your cells.
- **Red blood cells** make up just less than half your blood. Red blood cells carry oxygen to all the cells of your body. They pick up carbon dioxide from your cells and bring it to the lungs.
- **White blood cells** make up a small amount of your blood. They fight germs that enter the body.
- **Platelets** (PLAYT•lits) are small pieces of cells. They clump together to form a scab or clot when you cut yourself.

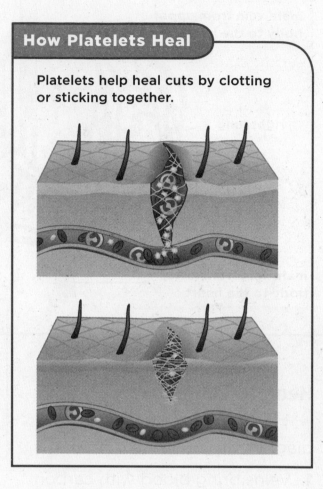

How Platelets Heal

Platelets help heal cuts by clotting or sticking together.

✓ Quick Check

Match the word and its description.

27. ___ red blood cells

28. ___ platelets

29. ___ white blood cells

a. fight germs

b. carry oxygen

c. forms clots

30. Why do you think there is so much plasma in your blood?

_____

_____

How do vessels and valves work?

Blood vessels form an unbroken path for blood.

- Arteries are thick-walled vessels leading away from the heart.
- Veins, which lead blood back to the heart, are thinner-walled. They are still thick enough to keep materials from passing through.
- Capillaries connect arteries to veins. They have thin walls. So nutrients can pass through the walls. So can oxygen and carbon dioxide.

Many veins have valves. These valves close up as needed to keep blood from backing up in the wrong direction. They then open to let blood flow in the correct direction.

Valves in the heart do much the same. They let blood flow from an atrium to a ventricle. However, they close to keep blood from flowing back in the wrong direction.

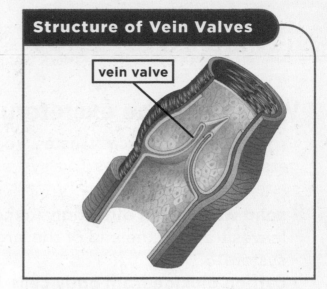

Structure of Vein Valves

vein valve

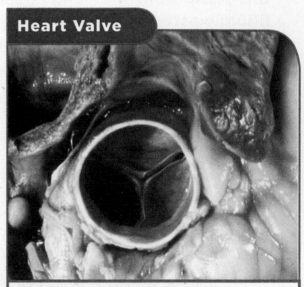

Heart Valve

Heart valves are like doors between chambers of the heart. They keep blood from flowing in the wrong direction.

 **Quick Check**

31. Why are valves important? _____

_____

32. Why does the body have three kinds of blood vessels? _____

_____

LOG ON e-Review Summaries and quizzes online @ **www.macmillanmh.com**

What does the excretory system do?

Your body produces wastes. Your excretory system gets rid of these wastes This system is really several systems:

- **solid waste from digestion** Remember, this waste leaves through the end of the large intestine (digestive system).
- **carbon dioxide from body cells** Remember, you exhale this waste from your lungs (respiratory system).
- **liquid wastes from body cells** The urinary (YUR•uh•ner•ee) system gets rid of these wastes:

1. These wastes are carried in the blood from the liver to the kidneys. The **kidneys** (KID•nees) are two bean-shaped organs that filter these wastes out of the blood.

2. The kidneys then produce urine (YUR•in). Urine is waste and water.

- **sweat** Sweat is water, salts, and wastes. It leaves your body through your skin system.

This lesson is about how urine and sweat leave the body.

✔ Quick Check

Fill in the diagram with the names of organ systems.

digestive	33. _____	34. _____	skin

Summary: The excretory system is made of several systems.

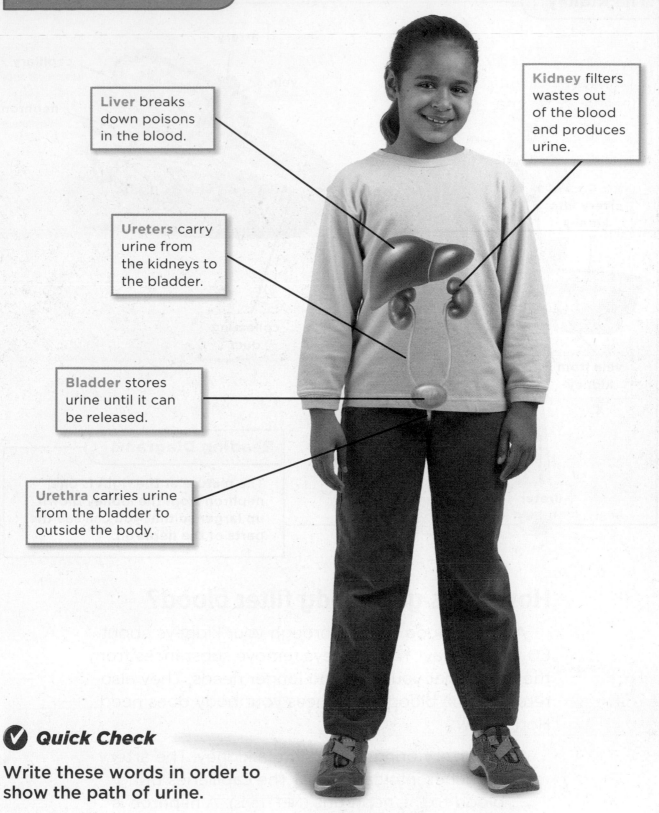

Liver breaks down poisons in the blood.

Kidney filters wastes out of the blood and produces urine.

Ureters carry urine from the kidneys to the bladder.

Bladder stores urine until it can be released.

Urethra carries urine from the bladder to outside the body.

✔ Quick Check

Write these words in order to show the path of urine.

bladder   urethra   ureters

35. _____

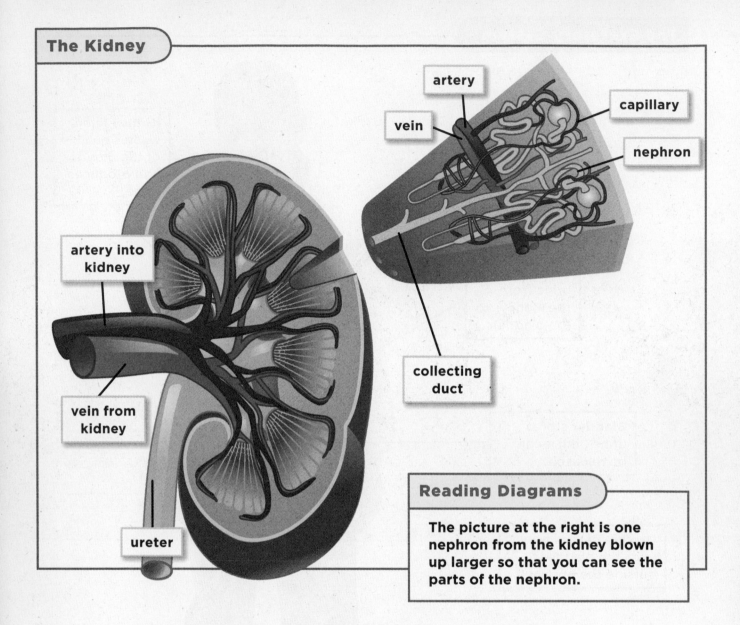

artery

vein

capillary

nephron

artery into kidney

vein from kidney

ureter

collecting duct

Reading Diagrams

The picture at the right is one nephron from the kidney blown up larger so that you can see the parts of the nephron.

How does your body filter blood?

All your blood passes through your kidneys about 60 times a day! Your kidneys remove substances from the blood that your body no longer needs. They also return to the blood substances your body does need. Here's how:

1. An artery brings blood into a kidney. The artery branches into capillaries. The capillaries bring blood to the nephrons (NEF•rons). A **nephron** is the part of a kidney where waste materials are separated from useful materials in the blood.

2. Wastes from the blood move out from the capillaries into the nephron. The wastes flow through a collecting duct. Collecting ducts from all the nephrons join into the ureter. The ureter leads the waste (urine) out of the kidney.

3. At the nephron, useful substances that may have been removed from the blood pass back into the capillaries. These capillaries lead blood to a vein. The vein carries the cleaned blood out of the kidney.

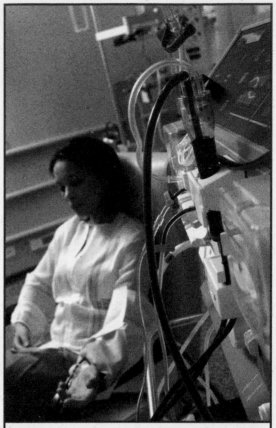

Dialysis removes dangerous wastes from this patient's blood.

What happens if the kidneys stop working?

Sometimes the kidneys may stop working properly. Wastes can build up in the blood to dangerous levels. People with this problem may need dialysis (digh•AL•uh•sis).

Dialysis is a treatment that uses a machine to do the job of the kidneys.

✔ Quick Check

36. How do wastes leave the kidney? _____

_____

37. How does cleaned blood leave the kidney? _____

_____

How does your body get rid of liquid wastes?

Your urinary system is like a drainage system. Your kidney collects wastes from the blood and forms urine.

- A tube called a ureter (yu•REE•tuhr) leads the urine out of the kidney
- The ureter brings urine into the bladder. Urine collects in the bladder for several hours.
- When the bladder is holding a lot of urine, eventually it is released into the urethra (yu•REE•thruh), The urethra carries urine from the bladder to outside the body.

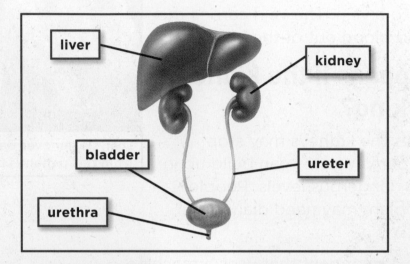

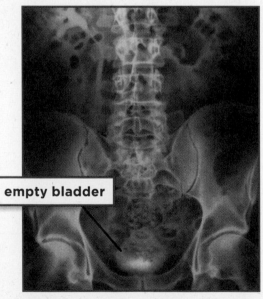

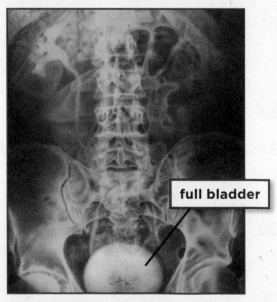

Empty, a bladder is about the size of a plum.

Full, it is about the size of a grapefruit.

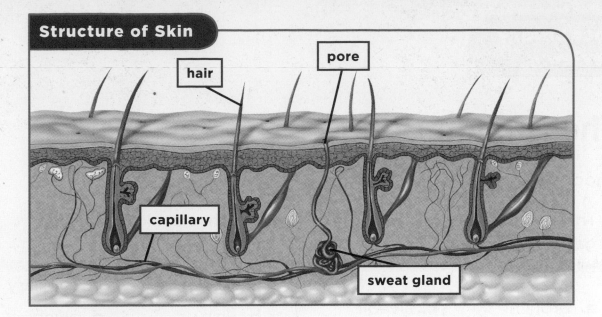

Structure of Skin

hair

pore

capillary

sweat gland

The Skin

Liquid waste also leaves your body through the skin. Sweat is made up of water, salts, and other wastes. Follow what happens in the skin diagram.

- Blood in the capillaries carries wastes. The wastes collect in a sweat gland.
- Sweat from the gland is pushed upward. It reaches the surface through an opening, called a pore (PAWR). At the surface it collects as droplets.
- The sweat evaporates from the surface. That is, the liquid turns into a gas and goes into the air. As the liquid turns into gas, it takes heat away from the skin. As heat is removed, your skin cools down.

✔ Quick Check

Match the word with its description.

38. ____ holds urine

a. pore

39. ____ opening in the skin

b. ureter

40. ____ leads urine out of the body

c. bladder

41. ____ brings urine to the bladder

d. urethra

LOG ON e-Review Summaries and quizzes online @ www.macmillanmh.com

The Human Body

Choose the letter of the best answer.

1. The air sacs in the lungs where gases move into and out of the blood are called

  a. bronchi   **c.** alveoli

  b. arteries   **d** veins

2. The thick tube-like organ that removes undigested waste is called the

  a. large intestine

  b. small intestine

  c. esophagus

  d. nephron

3. Breaking down food into simpler substances that your body can use is called

  a. respiration   **c.** transport

  b. breathing   **d.** digestion

4. The long muscular tube that brings food into the stomach is the

  a. diaphragm   **c.** kidney

  b. heart   **d.** esophagus

5. The thinnest kind of blood vessel is a(n)

  a. artery   **c.** capillary

  b. vein   **d.** alveoli

6. The part of the kidneys where waste materials are separated from useful materials in the blood is called the

  a. small intestine **c.** lung

  b. nephron   **d.** stomach

7. The organ that completes digestion and allows digested food to enter the blood is the

  a. small intestine

  b. bladder

  c. diaphragm

  d. saliva

8. A large, flat muscle that pulls air in and pushes air out of the lungs is the

  a. heart   **c.** diaphragm

  b. stomach   **d.** kidney

**Fill in the missing words. Fill in one letter for each blank.
Unscramble the numbered letters to answer the riddle below.**

1. A blood vessel that carries blood back to the heart is

   a(n) V E I N.
       1

2. A liquid that softens and moistens food in the mouth

   is S A L I V A.
      2

3. An organ that filters wastes from blood in the kidneys

   is a(n) N E P H R O N.
                  3

4. A blood vessel that carries blood away from

   the heart is a(n) A R T E R Y.
                     4   5

5. The two organs that fill up with air when you inhale are

   the L U N G S.
          6 7

6. The muscular organ that changes food into a thick, soupy

   liquid is the S T O M A C H.
                 8   9

7. The muscular organ that pumps blood throughout the

   body is the H E A R T.
               10   11

8. The organ that stores liquid wastes from the kidneys

   temporarily is the B L A D D E R.
                                12

Riddle: Who Are We?

We are made of body parts that have different jobs.

O R G A N   S Y S T E M S

CHAPTER 4

Earth's Water

Vocabulary

ocean a large body of salt water

fresh water water that has little or no salt

evaporation the changing of a liquid into gas

water vapor water in the form of an invisible, odorless gas

condensation the changing of a gas into liquid

precipitation droplets of water that form in the atmosphere and fall to the ground

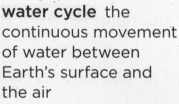
water cycle the continuous movement of water between Earth's surface and the air

reservoir a human-made lake that is used to store water

dam a barrier that prevents the normal flow of water

Where does the water you use come from?

groundwater water beneath Earth's surface

aquifer an underground layer of rock that can hold water

watershed the area where water drains into a river

flood the overflow of water from the banks of a body of water onto the land

drought a long period of dry weather

pollute to make dirty or unclean

reclamation making something usable again

aqueduct a pathway built by people to move water long distances

conserve save something to be sure there is enough

How much of Earth's surface is covered with water?

From California's coast, the Pacific Ocean stretches as far as you can see. An **ocean** is a large body of salt water. The map shows that most of Earth's surface, about 70%, is covered with oceans. The remaining 30% is mostly land, with some water on the land.

Oceans are very useful. They provide:

- food, such as fish, shrimp, and seaweed
- fuels, such as oil from the ocean bottom
- recreation and transportation

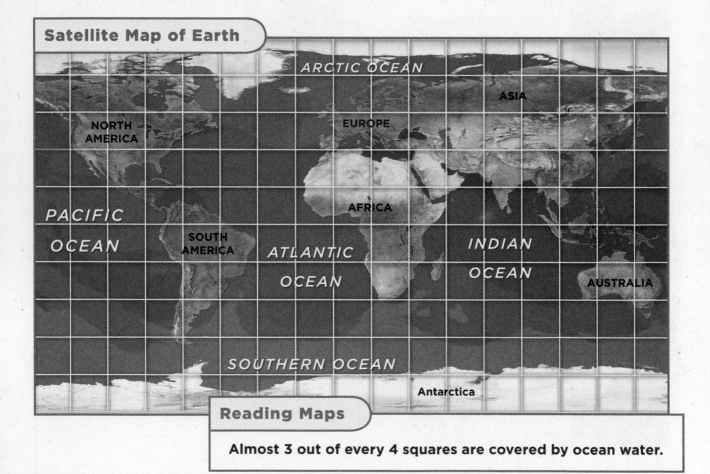

Satellite Map of Earth

ARCTIC OCEAN

ASIA

EUROPE

NORTH AMERICA

PACIFIC

OCEAN

SOUTH AMERICA

AFRICA

ATLANTIC

OCEAN

INDIAN

OCEAN

AUSTRALIA

SOUTHERN OCEAN

Antarctica

Reading Maps

Almost 3 out of every 4 squares are covered by ocean water.

Most of Earth's fresh water is frozen in Antarctica's huge ice sheet.

The World's Oceans

Ocean water flows uninterrupted around Earth. However, scientists have divided ocean water into several oceans because of the land between them, as well as how salty they are.

The biggest and deepest is the Pacific Ocean. One spot near the Philippine Islands is 11,033 meters (36,198 feet) deep. The Atlantic Ocean is only about half the size of the Pacific.

Fresh Water

The white covering on Greenland and Antarctica on the map represents huge sheets of ice. These ice sheets are made of fresh water. **Fresh water** contains little or no salt.

If 100 pennies represented all of Earth's water, only 1 penny, 1%, is fresh water. Most fresh water is frozen. The small amount of fresh water is found in rivers and lakes. However, Mono Lake contains salt water.

✔ Quick Check

Write *ocean water* or *fresh water* next to each description

1. most is frozen _____

2. covers about 70% of Earth _____

3. most lakes and rivers _____

4. provides fuels such as oil _____

rain

tributaries

river

What makes oceans salty?

Rain water falling on a mountain is fresh. However, as the water flows downhill, it picks up salt from soil and rocks.

The flowing water forms *tributaries* (TRIB•yuh•ter•eez). A tributary is a small river or stream that flows into a larger river. The larger river flows into the ocean. River water does not taste salty because it has a small amount of salt. However, it carries the salt into the ocean all the time.

Along a coast, waves pound on rocks and sand. The pounding waves pick up salt, adding salt to the oceans.

Salt Does Not Evaporate

Reading Diagrams

What is the path of water as it collects salt on the way to the ocean?

LOG ON *Science in Motion* Watch water flow to the ocean @ **www.macmillanmh.com**

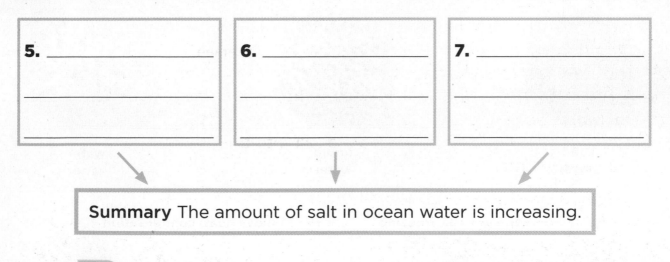

ocean

evaporate

Sunlight shines on the oceans. Water at the surface is heated. This heat causes evaporation (i•vap•uh•RAY•shuhn). **Evaporation** is the changing of a liquid to a gas. Water at the surface of the ocean is slowly changing to a gas, water vapor. **Water vapor** is water in the form of a gas. You can't see it or taste it.

As liquid water turns into water vapor, it rises out of the ocean. It goes into the air. The salt stays behind. The remaining water becomes saltier and saltier.

Today, every 100 grams (3.5 ounces) of ocean water holds about 3.5 grams (0.12 ounces) of salts.

✔ Quick Check

Fill in the diagram. List ways that ocean water is made more and more salty.

5. _____

6. _____

7. _____

Summary The amount of salt in ocean water is increasing.

LOG ON **e-Review** Summaries and quizzes online @ **www.macmillanmh.com**

What makes water change form?

You may think of water as only a liquid. However, water can be in three forms, or states:

- solid (ice)
- liquid (water in a glass or lake)
- water vapor (invisible gas in the air)

Water can change states. Start with ice, such as ice on a pond in winter. When the pond heats up in spring and summer, the ice melts. It becomes liquid. Heat can also make liquid water in the pond change to water vapor.

Heat is removed as the pond and the air above it get colder from summer to fall and winter. Water vapor in cooled air turns back into liquid and can fall as rain or snow. Changing a gas to a liquid is **condensation** (con•den•SAY•shuhn). As months get colder, more heat is removed from the pond. The pond freezes again.

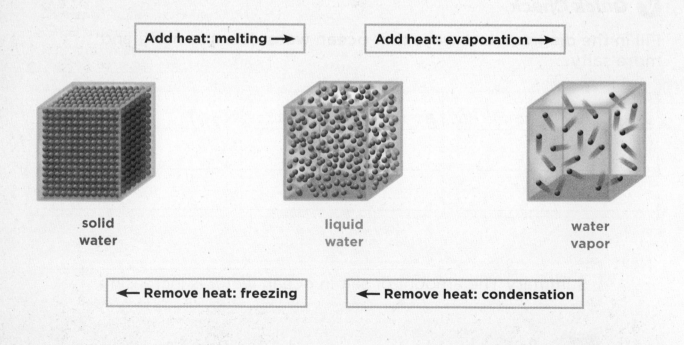

Add heat: melting ➡   Add heat: evaporation ➡

solid water   liquid water   water vapor

⬅ Remove heat: freezing   ⬅ Remove heat: condensation

Changes in State of Water in a Pond

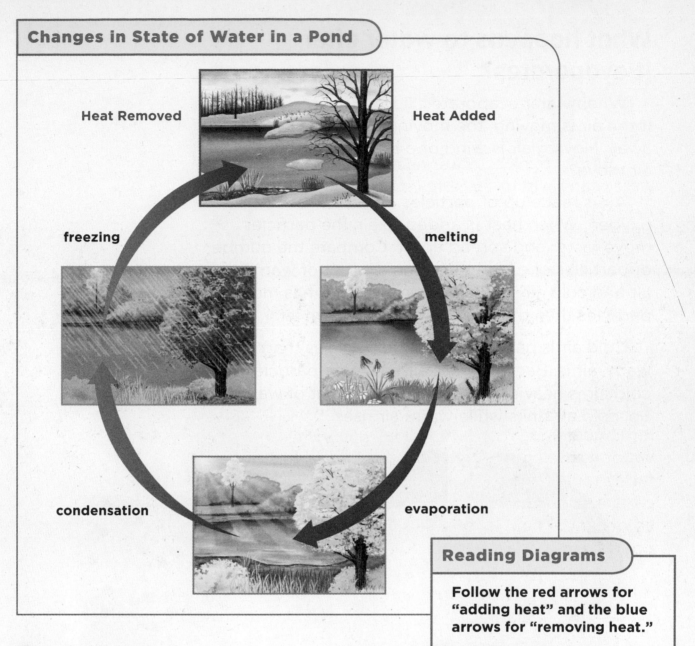

Heat Removed

Heat Added

freezing

melting

condensation

evaporation

Reading Diagrams

Follow the red arrows for "adding heat" and the blue arrows for "removing heat."

✓ *Quick Check*

Fill in the diagram. What happens as heat added to ice?

First   ice

Next **8.** _____

Last **9.** _____

What happens to water after it evaporates?

When water evaporates, it goes up into the air. If the air is moving, the moving air can carry it away. Moving air is wind or a breeze. What makes air move?

Air is made up of particles of gases, such as oxygen. When heat is added to air, the particles move faster and spread apart. Compare the number of particles of gas in the same amount of warm air and cold air in the diagram. Cold air has more particles than the same amount of warm air.

Cold air is packed with more particles than the warm air is. Because cold air has more particles in it, cold air is heavier than an equal amount of warm air. So, cold air sinks while warm air rises.

Large balloons can rise into the air because air inside of them is heated.

warm air

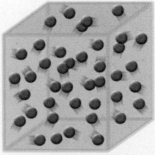

cold air

At the shore during the day, sunlight warms land and water. Land warms up faster than water does.

- As land heats up, air above it gets warmer. Warm air over land rises.
- Air over water sinks. It moves toward land to replace the rising warm air. A *sea breeze* is felt moving from water to land.

Sea Breezes

warm air   cold air

At night along the shore, land and water cool off. Land cools faster than water.

- Air stays warmer longer over water. Warm air over water rises.
- Air over land cools faster than air over water. Air sinks over land and moves toward water. A *land breeze* is felt moving from land toward water.

Land Breezes

warm air   cold air

✔ Quick Check

Write **warm air** or **cool air** in each space.

10. rises _____

11. particles of gas move apart _____

12. over water at night _____

13. over water during the day _____

How do clouds form?

The air around you may look empty. However it is not. It is filled with invisible particles of gases, such as oxygen. It also contains invisible particles of water vapor. Remember, water vapor is water in the form of a gas.

The water vapor is produced when liquid water is heated. Evaporation takes place. Particles of water vapor rise and slowly lose heat energy. They become colder and get closer together.

Eventually, condensation takes place. The particles of water vapor collect around dust in the air. When they collect, they form droplets of liquid water. You have seen these droplets form on a cold glass or window.

When more and more droplets of water collect, you eventually see a cloud. The more droplets there are, the larger the cloud becomes.

How Clouds Form

condensation

evaporation

✔ Quick Check

14. What causes condensation of water vapor? _____

_____

_____

Different Kinds of Clouds

Clouds come in different shapes. Their shape depends on how high they form in the sky and what the temperature is. Air is colder higher up than closer to the ground.

Cirrus clouds, for example, form high in the sky. They are made of bits of ice. The bits of ice form when liquid water in the air is cooled below the freezing point, 0°C (32°F). It may be so cold that water vapor turns into ice without becoming liquid water first.

Lower clouds are made of water droplets. They may look dark because they are so crowded with droplets. *Fog* is a cloud that forms near the ground.

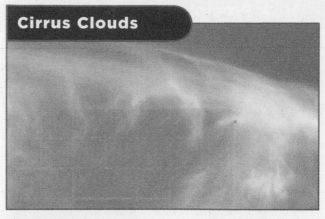
Cirrus Clouds

Cirrus clouds form high in the sky. They are thin and wispy.

Cumulus Clouds

Cumulus clouds are puffy and seem to rise up from a flat bottom.

Stratus Clouds

Stratus clouds are low-lying clouds that spread like a blanket across the sky.

✓ *Quick Check*

15. List these clouds in order from highest to lowest: stratus   fog   cirrus.

_____

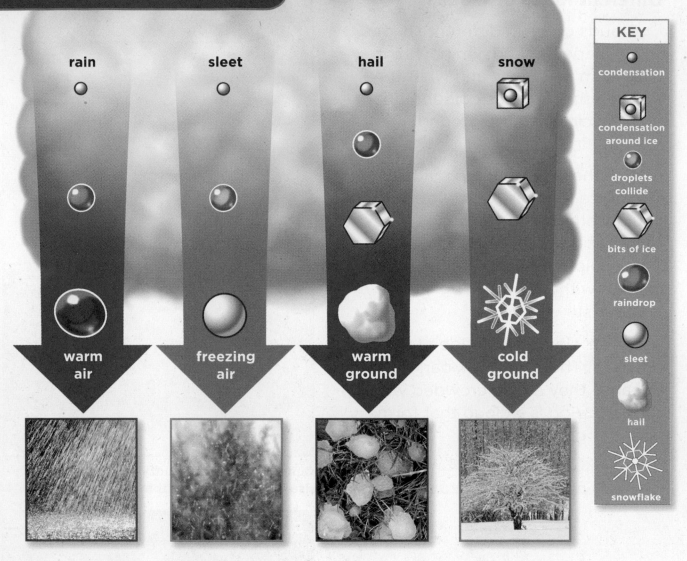

KEY

○	condensation
⬚	condensation around ice
●	droplets collide
⬡	bits of ice
●	raindrop
●	sleet
●	hail
❋	snowflake

rain — warm air

sleet — freezing air

hail — warm ground

snow — cold ground

Will it rain?

When clouds are made up of liquid drops (instead of bits of ice), the drops start to fall of their own weight. Wind pushes them back up and they join together into heavier drops. In time, the drops are so large and heavy, they fall to the ground as precipitation (pri•sip•i•TAY•shuhn). **Precipitation** is water that falls from the air. It can be rain, sleet, hail, or snow.

Rain falls when:

- air up above the ground is cool enough for condensation to take place.
- the drops fall through air that is warmer than the freezing point of water, 0°C (32°F), or the air just above the ground is warmer than freezing.

Sleet, Hail, Snow

Sleet falls when

- air up above the ground is cool enough for condensation to take place.
- the drops freeze as they fall through very cold air and reach very cold temperatures near the ground.

Hail falls when

- drops of water and ice in a cloud collide. The drops freeze onto the ice, forming a hailstone.
- winds in the cloud keep pushing the hailstone back up. The hailstone gets larger until it falls.

Snow falls when

- the temperature up in the sky is cold enough for water vapor to turn directly into solid flakes. It does not form liquid drops first.
- the snowflakes fall through cold air and reach very cold surfaces at the ground.

How Hailstones Form

1 Strong winds move drops of water and ice around in a cloud.

2 The water and ice collide and form hailstones.

3 Upward moving winds push falling hailstones back up into the cloud.

4 Hailstones get larger as more drops of water freeze onto them.

5 Hailstones fall to the ground.

✔ Quick Check

Match the word and the description.

16. ____ rain falls through cold air

17. ____ water vapor forms ice

18. ____ wind pushes ice balls up

19. ____ water falls through warm air

a. hail

b. rain

c. snow

d. sleet

How is water recycled?

Water on Earth is never lost. Water keeps changing from solid to liquid to gas and then back to liquid and solid. It keeps moving from Earth's surface to the sky and then back to Earth. The continuous movement of water between Earth's surface and the sky as it changes form is called the **water cycle**.

The Water Cycle

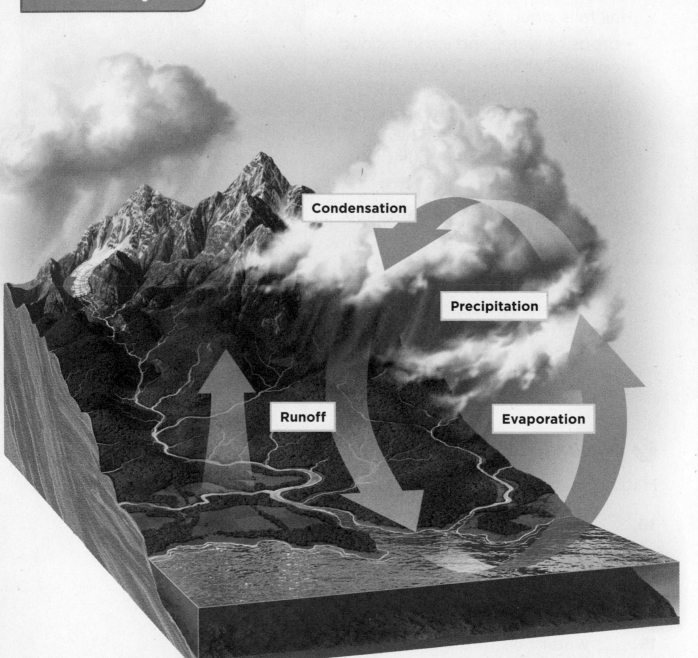

Condensation

Precipitation

Runoff

Evaporation

How the Cycle Works

The water cycle has no beginning or end. To read the diagram, pick a place to start—such as *evaporation*—and follow the arrows.

- **evaporation** Water from Earth's surface turns into water vapor and rises into the air.

- **condensation** As water vapor reaches colder air in the sky, it turns into drops of liquid water (or bits of ice). Clouds form.

- **precipitation** Rain, sleet, hail, or snow falls to Earth's surface.

- **runoff** Fallen water or melted snow may soak into the ground. However, much of it runs over the ground. It collects into rivers, which bring water to the ocean. The cycle keeps going.

✔ Quick Check

Fill in the diagram with the four steps of the water cycle. Be sure they are in order.

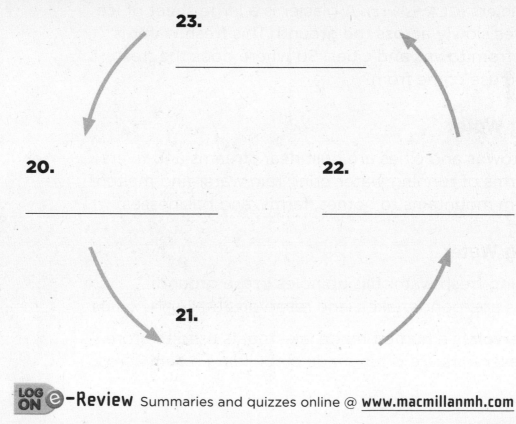

23. _____

20. _____

22. _____

21. _____

LOG ON ⓔ **-Review** Summaries and quizzes online @ **www.macmillanmh.com**

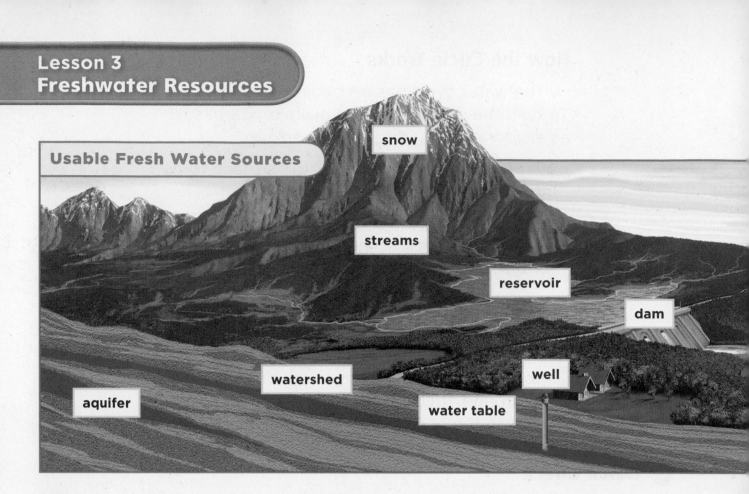

Usable Fresh Water Sources

snow

streams

reservoir

dam

watershed

well

aquifer

water table

Where is freshwater found?

Much of Earth's fresh water is frozen in huge sheets of ice or glaciers (GLAY•shurz). A glacier is a large sheet of ice that moves slowly across the ground. This fresh water is far away from towns and cities. So where does the fresh water you use come from?

Running Water

Most towns and cities are built near streams and rivers. These forms of running water bring rain water and melted snow from mountains to homes, farms, and businesses.

Standing Water

Standing fresh water fills up holes in the ground. Examples are, ponds, lakes, and reservoirs (REZ•uhr•vwahrs).

A **reservoir** is a human-made lake that is used to store water. Reservoirs are often made by building a **dam** across a river.

Reading Diagrams

Read and compare the labels. Look for two human-made structures that are used to get fresh water.

river

lake

Groundwater

Many towns, farms, and factories depend on **groundwater**, water beneath the surface. As rainwater seeps down into the ground, it eventually reaches a layer of rock that it cannot seep through. Groundwater builds up above that layer, forming a water table.

Groundwater may collect in an aquifer (AK•wuh•fuhr). An **aquifer** is an underground layer of rock or soil that holds water. People dig wells to reach an aquifer or the water table.

✓ Quick Check

Explain what the words in each set have in common.

24. wells, dams _____

_____

25. aquifer, water table _____

_____

What is a watershed?

Each day, about 16 trillion liters (4.2 trillion gallons) of rain water falls on the United States. Three things happen to this water:

- two-thirds of it evaporates back into the air
- a small amount seeps into the ground
- the rest runs over land and drains into rivers.

The area of land in which water drains into a river is called a **watershed**. As water flows through a watershed:

- it replaces water that rivers and lakes lose through evaporation
- some of it seeps into the ground and adds to the supply of groundwater
- it fills water sources for people.

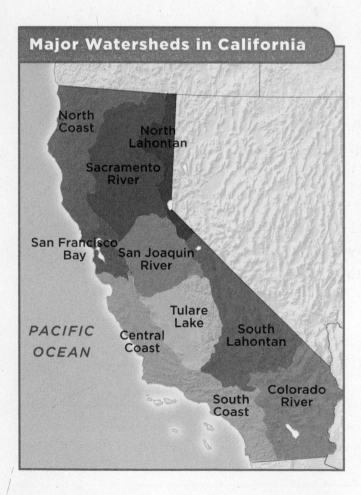

Major Watersheds in California

North Coast

North Lahontan

Sacramento River

San Francisco Bay

San Joaquin River

Tulare Lake

South Lahontan

PACIFIC OCEAN

Central Coast

South Coast

Colorado River

Watersheds in Central Valley

Towns and farms are found in watersheds.

Water can cover the land for days after a flood.

The Flow of Water

Plants help control the flow of water in a watershed. Roots grow down and hold soil in place. Soil with roots can soak up water that runs downhill. If plants are removed, such as by building roads or sidewalks, water can flow faster and carry away soil.

Fast-flowing water can enter a river faster than the river can carry it away. A flood can happen. A **flood** is the pouring of water over the banks of a body of water and spreading over the land. Floods carry away things and cover streets and homes with water.

On the other hand, during dry periods, streams that feed watersheds may dry up. People who rely on these streams face a water shortage.

✔ *Quick Check*

26. Why are towns and farms built in watersheds? _____

_____

27. What may happen when trees are cleared in a watershed?

_____

_____

How is water polluted?

As water runs over land, it soaks up substances that pollute (puh•LEWT) the water. To **pollute** means to "dirty." Water soaks up

- chemicals used to help crops to grow
- chemicals used to kill harmful insects
- waste products from farms and factories
- spilled motor oils and trash.

Polluted water flows into rivers. It soaks into groundwater. Water can be unsafe to use.

Water can be so polluted that almost nothing can live in it.

Laws

City and state governments pass laws to try to keep water safe. The U.S. government passed:

- Safe Drinking Water Act of 1974, which sets rules for keeping water safe to drink
- Clean Water Act of 1977, which made it illegal to pollute water.

✓ Quick Check

28. How can water become polluted? _____

_____

_____

29. Why do you think it is illegal to pollute water? _____

_____

_____

How is water cleaned?

Water that reaches homes and businesses has been cleaned in water treatment plants. Some of the steps used to clean water are:

- *coagulation* (koh•AG•yew•lay•shuhn) Sticky particles are added to clump dirt together.
- *sedimentation* (sed•i•men•TAY•shuhn) Clumped dirt falls to the bottom of a tank.
- *filtration* (fil•TRAY•shuhn) Water passes through screens that trap soil and dirt.
- *disinfection* (DIS•in•fek•shuhn) Chemicals are added to kill harmful bacteria.

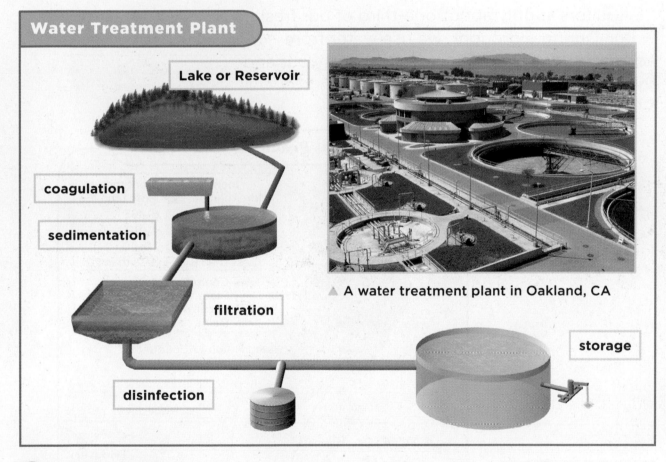

Water Treatment Plant

Lake or Reservoir

coagulation

sedimentation

filtration

disinfection

storage

▲ A water treatment plant in Oakland, CA

✔ Quick Check

30. Why are so many steps used to clean water? _____

_____

LOG ON **e-Review** Summaries and quizzes online @ **www.macmillanmh.com**

Where is our fresh water from?

Most rain falls in the northern part of our state. However, most people live in the southern part. The greatest need for water is where rain falls the least. See the map.

The supply of water decreases when there is a drought (DROUT). A **drought** is a long period of dry weather.

Aquifers supply about one-third of our fresh water. During a drought, we use water from aquifers even more. Aquifers can empty out and the ground above them may collapse.

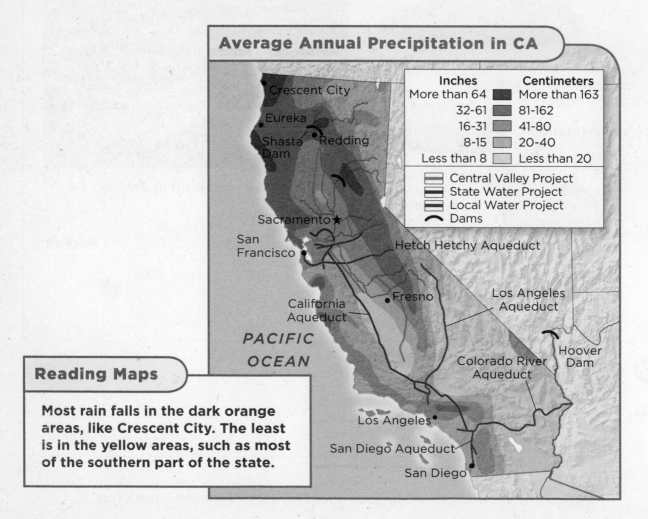

Average Annual Precipitation in CA

Inches		Centimeters
More than 64		More than 163
32-61		81-162
16-31		41-80
8-15		20-40
Less than 8		Less than 20

Central Valley Project
State Water Project
Local Water Project
Dams

Crescent City
Eureka
Shasta Dam Redding
Sacramento ★
San Francisco
Hetch Hetchy Aqueduct
California Aqueduct
Fresno
Los Angeles Aqueduct
PACIFIC OCEAN
Colorado River Aqueduct
Hoover Dam
Los Angeles
San Diego Aqueduct
San Diego

Reading Maps

Most rain falls in the dark orange areas, like Crescent City. The least is in the yellow areas, such as most of the southern part of the state.

Reclaiming Used Water

Much used water in our state is run through reclamation (re•kluh•MAY•shuhn) plants. **Reclamation** means to make usable again. Water reclamation plants filter and clean used water. One use of the cleaned used water is to refill drying aquifers. Then the water table goes up and wells can fill with groundwater.

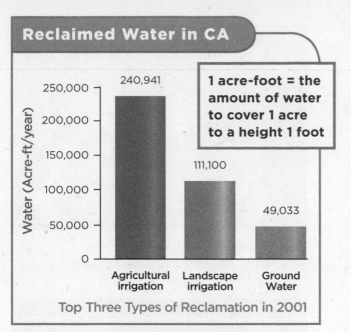

Reclaimed Water in CA

1 acre-foot = the amount of water to cover 1 acre to a height 1 foot

Water (Acre-ft/year)

250,000 — 240,941
200,000
150,000
100,000 — 111,100
50,000 — 49,033
0

Agricultural irrigation | Landscape irrigation | Ground Water

Top Three Types of Reclamation in 2001

Source: *California State Water Resources Control Board, Office of Water Recycling*

The Sangus Water Reclamation Plant in Santa Clarita cleans 7 million gallons of used water each day.

✔ Quick Check

31. Read the map. Two cities that get 20–40 centimeters of precipitation

are _____

_____

32. Read the graph. The smallest amount of water reclamation is from

_____.

How is our fresh water supplied?

Local, state, and federal governments have built ways to store and move fresh water in our state. Dams were built to hold river water in reservoirs. Water is then moved throughout the state through aqueducts (AK•kwee•dukts). An **aqueduct** is a channel built by people to move water long distances.

For example, the California Aqueduct is part of the State Water Project. The U.S. government built the Central Valley Project, which includes the Shasta Dam. Care is taken to protect the environment from which the water is taken.

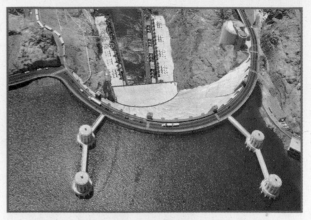

The Hoover Dam blocks the river and forms a reservoir, Lake Mead.

Water from Lake Mead travels through the Los Angeles Aqueduct.

✔ Quick Check

Fill in the diagram. Name two things built by people to store and move water.

Main Idea	Details
People store and move water.	33. _____
	34. _____

How can we save water?

A little more than half the water we get in our state soaks into the ground, evaporates, and is used by plants. The rest, a little less than half, is used for cites, farms, and the environment. The environment includes water in rivers and lakes.

To be sure we have enough water, many people try to save, that is, **conserve** water. For example, to save water when we water lawns, we can grow plants that use less water.

WATER USE IN HOMES

Bathroom
Showers 16.8%
Baths: 1.7%
Toilets 13.7%
Kitchen
Faucets 15.7%
Dishwasher 1.4%
Other uses 2.2%
Basement
Leaks 13.7%
Washing Machine 13%
Laundry Room

Source: *American Water Works Association*

Supply and Uses	Wet year (1998)	Normal year (2000)	Dry year (2001)
Total water supply	336.9	194.7	145.5
Use by cities	7.8	8.9	8.6
Use by farms	27.3	34.2	33.7
Environmental uses	59.4	39.4	22.5

Source: *California Water Plan Update* Units: million acre-feet

✓ Quick Check

35. Which use of water did not change much in any year in the chart? Why? _____

_____

36. Based on the diagram, how might you conserve water at home?

_____

_____

Earth's Water

fresh water	evaporation	water vapor	condensation
precipitation	water cycle	groundwater	watershed
reclamation	aqueduct		

Use a word from the box to name each example described below.

1. the area where water drains into a river _____

2. water that has little or no salt _____

3. droplets of water that form in the air and fall

to the ground _____

4. a pathway built by people to move water long distances

_____

5. the continuous movement of water between Earth's surface

and the air _____

6. water beneath Earth's surface _____

7. making something usable again _____

8. the changing of a liquid into gas _____

9. water in the form of an invisible, odorless gas

_____

10. water that has little or no salt _____

Answer the riddle. Use the words from the box at the top of the page.

11. Which word in the box includes two of the other words? Explain.

_____

_____

Read each clue. Use the answers to fill in the crossword puzzle.

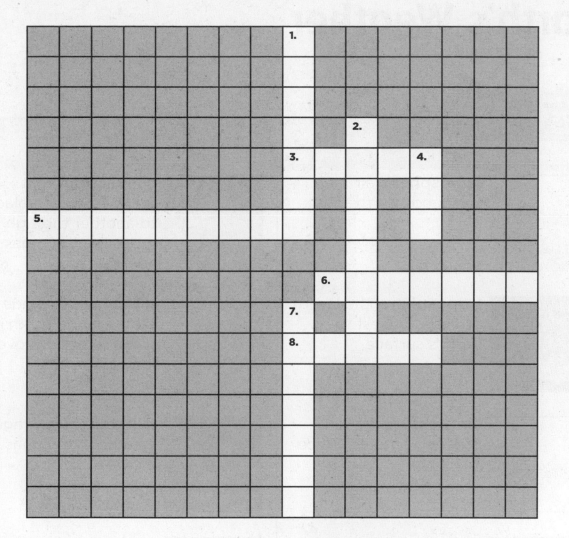

Across

3. the overflow of water from the banks of a body of water onto the land

5. a human-made lake that is used to store water

6. a long period of dry weather

8. a large body of salt water

Down

1. an underground layer of rock that can hold water

2. to save something to be sure there is enough

4. a barrier that prevents the normal flow of water

7. to make dirty or unclean

CHAPTER 5

Earth's Weather

Vocabulary

atmosphere air that surrounds Earth

troposphere the layer of gases closest to Earth's surface

air pressure air pressing onto a surface

humidity water vapor in the air

air and water vapor

barometer a tool that measures air pressure

convection heat going from one place to another through movement of a gas or liquid

global wind winds that blow around Earth in given directions over long distances

climate the average weather conditions of a place

current the ongoing movement of ocean water

air mass a large amount of air that has similar temperature and humidity throughout

How can we tell what the weather will be?

front a meeting place between two air masses

thunderstorm a rainstorm that includes lightning and thunder

tornado a spinning funnel cloud that has winds up to 480 kilometers (299 miles) per hour

cyclone a storm with low pressure at its center and spinning winds

hurricane a large spinning storm that has winds over 117 kilometers (73 miles) per hour

storm surge a large rise in the height of ocean water caused by a hurricane

forecast to make a guess about what may happen based on careful observation

weather map a map that shows weather conditions over an area at a given time

What is air pressure?

Air looks empty. However, you can feel gases in air when you wave your hand. You can see the gases fill a tire. Air is made of gases, mostly nitrogen and oxygen.

The air that surrounds Earth is called the **atmosphere** (AT•muhs•feer). It reaches from Earth up to about 700 kilometers (435 miles).

The atmosphere is made up of five layers. The layer closest to the Earth is the **troposphere** (TROP•uh•sfeer). Weather happens here. Here gases in the air are most crowded together. Higher up, gases thin out.

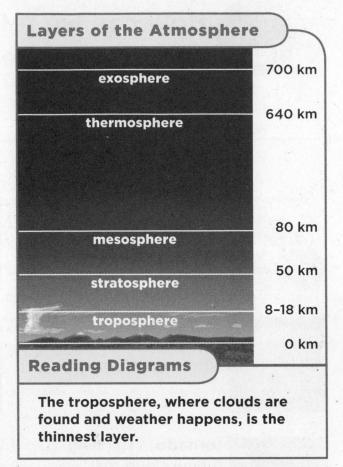

Layers of the Atmosphere

exosphere	700 km
thermosphere	640 km
mesosphere	80 km
stratosphere	50 km
troposphere	8–18 km
	0 km

Reading Diagrams

The troposphere, where clouds are found and weather happens, is the thinnest layer.

▲ Earth's atmosphere reaches from Earth's surface about 700 kilometers into space.

Air Pressing Down

All the air in the atmosphere presses onto Earth's surface. The amount of air pressing onto an area is called **air pressure**.

Think of air pressure as the weight of a column of air pressing down on a patch of Earth's surface. At "sea level" on Earth's surface, a little over 1 kilogram of air presses down onto each square centimeter (almost 15 pounds for each square inch). That is the air pressure at "sea level."

High on a mountaintop, the column of air pressing down is shorter. So it weighs less. There is less air pressure as you climb up.

You don't feel this pressure because air pressure pushes in on you in all directions. These pushes balance each other out.

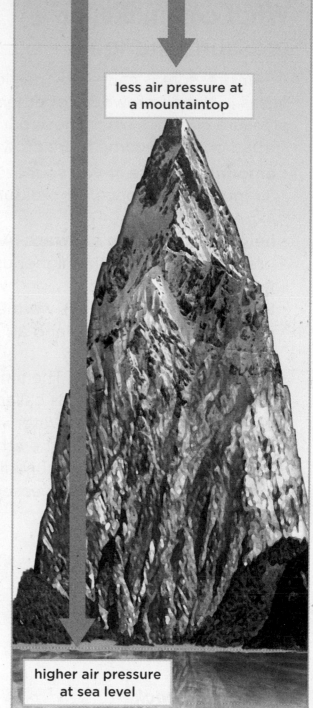

less air pressure at a mountaintop

higher air pressure at sea level

The lengths of the arrows help you compare the air pressure on the two places. There is less air pressure at a mountain than at sea level. ▶

✔ Quick Check

1. How can you tell that there is air around you? _____

_____

2. What causes air pressure? _____

_____

What can make air pressure change?

Air pressure is caused by particles of gases in the air crowded together. Air pressure changes when these particles spread out or become more crowded.

- **amount of space** If you squeeze air into a small space, air pressure *increases*.
- **height above Earth's surface** Air pressure *decreases* the higher up you go.
- **temperature** When air is warmed, the particles spread out and air pressure *decreases*.
- **amount of water vapor** The amount of water vapor in the air is called **humidity** (hew•MID•i•tee). Water vapor weighs less than most of the other gases in the air. So when humidity increases, air pressure *decreases*.

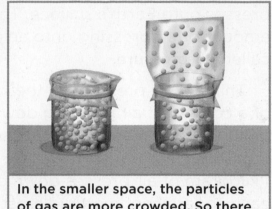

In the smaller space, the particles of gas are more crowded. So there is more air pressure.

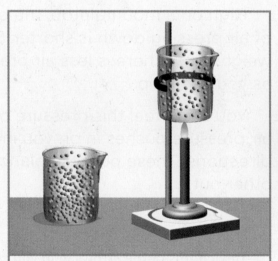

In the heated gas, the particles move apart and are less crowed. So warming air decreases air pressure.

✔ Quick Check

Write *decreases* or *increases* in each blank.

3. When air gets warmer, air pressure _____.

4. When air is squeezed into a small space, air pressure

_____.

5. When humidity increases, air pressure _____.

What is a barometer?

Air pressure can change during any day. For example, air pressure changes when air temperature changes. Tools called **barometers** (buh•ROM•i•turs) are used to measure air pressure and tell how it changes.

There are two kinds of barometers.

- **mercury** Air pressure pushes onto mercury in a tube. Mecury is a liquid metal. As air pressure increases, the mercury rises in the tube.
- **aneroid** (A•nuh•royd) Air pressure pushes onto an airtight container. The container gets smaller as air pressure increases.

Pilots use barometers to tell how high up their planes are. The higher up they are, the lower the air pressure is.

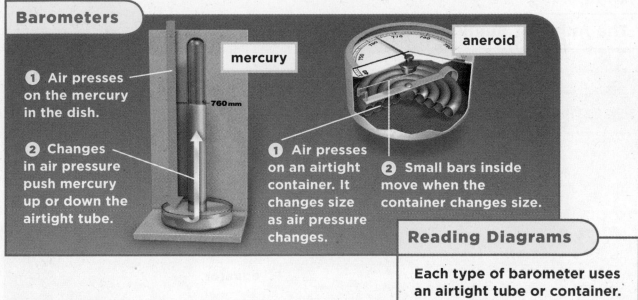

Barometers

mercury

aneroid

1. Air presses on the mercury in the dish.

—760mm

2. Changes in air pressure push mercury up or down the airtight tube.

1. Air presses on an airtight container. It changes size as air pressure changes.

2. Small bars inside move when the container changes size.

Reading Diagrams

Each type of barometer uses an airtight tube or container.

✅ Quick Check

Describe how a barometer changes in each case.

6. When air pressure increases, the mercury _____.

7. When air pressure decreases, the size of the airtight container _____

_____.

LOG ON **e–Review** Summaries and quizzes online @ **www.macmillanmh.com**

Why are temperatures different?

One year, on the first day of spring, the temperature in Seattle, Washington was 10°C (50°F). At the same time, the temperature in San Diego, California, was higher, 25°C (77°F). At any one time, air temperature is different in different places all around Earth. Why?

One reason is Earth's shape. Earth is shaped like a ball. Because of Earth's ball-shape, sunlight is more direct in some places and more slanted in others. For example, it is most direct at the *equator* (i•KWAY•tuhr). The equator is an imaginary line around Earth's middle.

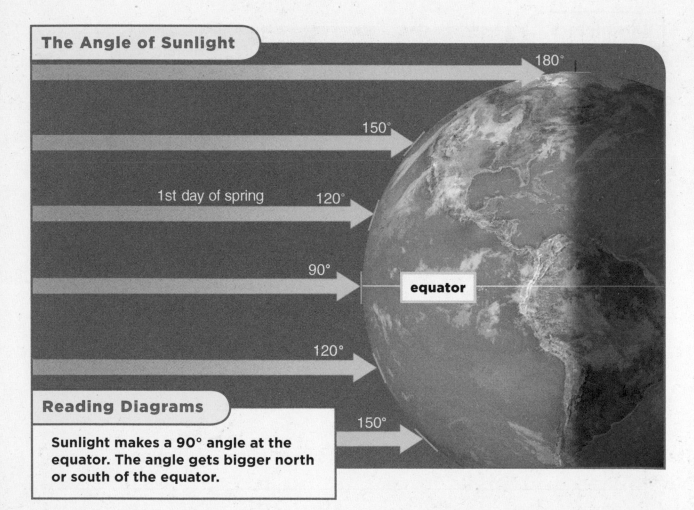

The Angle of Sunlight

180°

150°

1st day of spring   120°

90°   equator

120°

Reading Diagrams

Sunlight makes a 90° angle at the equator. The angle gets bigger north or south of the equator.

150°

Direct and Slanted

The circles below help you compare direct and slanted beams of light. The most direct beam of light (90°) is a small circle. This circle focuses all its energy on a small spot. This spot gets warmer than light from slanted beams.

Slanted beams of light spread out when they reach Earth. They are ovals of light at 120° and 150°. At 180° the light spreads way out. When light spreads out over an area, that place warms up less than when light is more direct.

Places closer to the equator get more direct light. So places like San Diego get more direct heat from the Sun and are warmer than places to the north (like Seattle) or south.

90° sunlight

120° sunlight

150° sunlight

180° sunlight

Seattle

San Diego

▲ Sun's rays are more direct at San Diego than to the north, at Seattle.

✔ Quick Check

Match the shape of the sunbeam at each angle.

8. ____ 180°   **a.** circle

9. ____ 120°   **b.** spreads way out in all directions

10. ____ 90°   **c.** an oval

How is air pressure different over land and water?

During the day along a shore, you can feel a *sea breeze* coming from the sea toward land.

At night or early in the morning, you feel a *land breeze* moving from land out to sea. Why?

Sea Breeze During the day land heats up faster than water. Water stays cooler longer.

- As air over the land gets warmer, air pressure over the land drops. Air pressure over the water stays higher longer.
- The sea breeze moves from high pressure over the water to low pressure over the land. That is, the sea breeze moves:

High ⟶ Low

Air Pressure in a Sea Breeze

high pressure

cold air

low pressure

warm air

A sea breeze moves from high to low pressure.

Land Breeze At night land cools off faster than water. Air over the water stays warm longer.

- As air over the land gets cooler, air pressure over the land rises. Air pressure over the water is lower.
- So the land breeze moves from high pressure over land to lower pressure over water. That is, the sea breeze moves:

High ⟶ Low

Air Pressure in a Land Breeze

high pressure

cold air

low pressure

warm air

A land breeze moves from high to low pressure.

✔ *Quick Check*

Compare sea and land breezes.

Sea breeze (different)   **alike**   **Land breeze** (different)

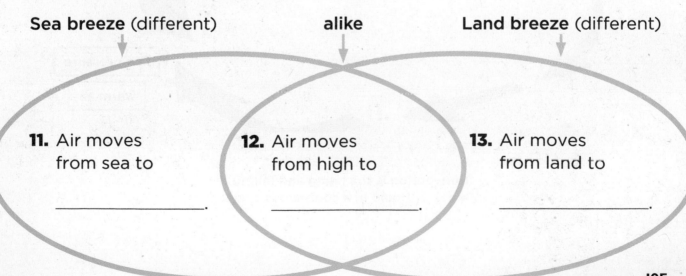

11. Air moves from sea to

_____.

12. Air moves from high to

_____.

13. Air moves from land to

_____.

What are global winds?

Land and water temperatures change throughout the day because land warms up faster than water does. The changes in air temperature cause air pressure to change as well. As temperature goes up, air pressure goes down. As temperature goes down, air pressure goes up.

Convection

Air always moves from areas of high pressure to areas of low pressure. In areas of high pressure, cool air is sinking. In areas of low pressure, warm air is rising. So as air moves, heat is traveling along with the air.

Heat traveling through the movement of a gas or liquid is **convection** (con•VEK•shuhn). When convection happens in air, it forms winds. These can be just local breezes or winds around the world.

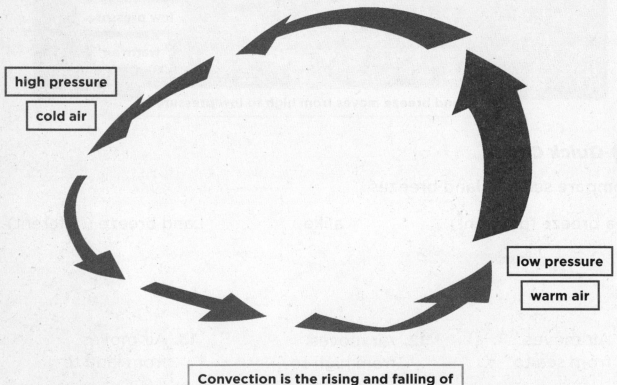

high pressure

cold air

low pressure

warm air

Convection is the rising and falling of a gas or liquid in a continuous cycle.

Trade Winds

Sailors who traveled from Europe to the Americas years ago used winds that always blow from northeast to southwest.

They found these winds between the Tropic of Cancer and the equator, the *trade winds*.

Remember, the equator has low pressure because sunlight heats the equator directly. *Trade winds* blow all the time from higher pressure at the tropics to the equator.

Trade winds are part of a system of winds blowing all around Earth, the **global winds**. Global winds blow in predictable directions over long distances all the time. They always blow from high to low pressure.

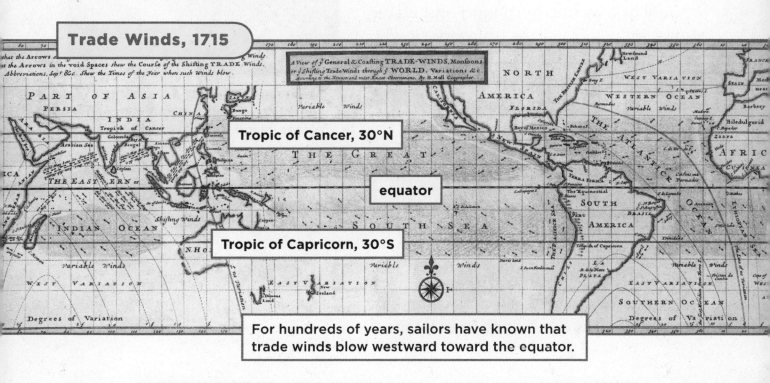

Trade Winds, 1715

Tropic of Cancer, 30°N

equator

Tropic of Capricorn, 30°S

For hundreds of years, sailors have known that trade winds blow westward toward the equator.

✓ Quick Check

14. In all winds, air moves from _____ pressure

to _____ pressure.

15. Trade winds move from the tropics to _____.

LOG ON **e-Review** Summaries and quizzes online @ **www.macmillanmh.com**

How do oceans affect temperature on land?

If you live along the coast, air temperatures are different from places inland. In winter it is warmer near the coast and colder inland. In summer it is cooler near the coast and warmer inland. Why?

Sunlight warms both land and water. However, water warms up more slowly than land. That is, water stays cooler longer than land. The air above the water also stays cooler longer.

- So in the summer, in places near water, air temperatures are lower than places inland.

In winter water cools off more slowly than land does. That is, water stays warmer than land, and so does the air above the water.

- So in winter, in places near water, air temperatures are higher than inland.

▲ Areas near the coast have warmer winters and cooler summers than places inland.

	summer	winter
water	warms up slowly (lower temperatures)	cools off slowly (higher temperatures)
inland	warms up faster (higher temperatures)	cools off faster (lower temperatures)

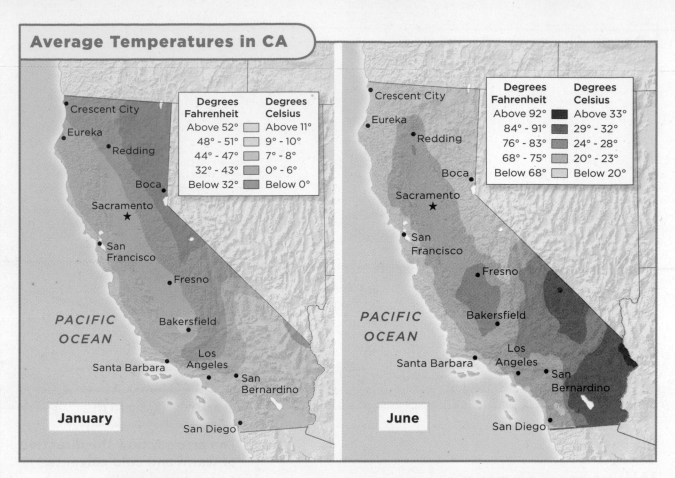

Climate

Around the world places near oceans feel the same effect. Coastal areas are cooler in the summer and warmer in the winter compared with places inland.

Coastal areas have a milder climate (KLIGH•mit) than places inland. **Climate** is the average weather conditions of a place. Climate includes average temperatures and rainfall.

✓ Quick Check

16. Compare the temperatures in two cities on the map.

	January	June
Santa Barbara	a. _____	b. _____
San Bernadino	c. _____	d. _____

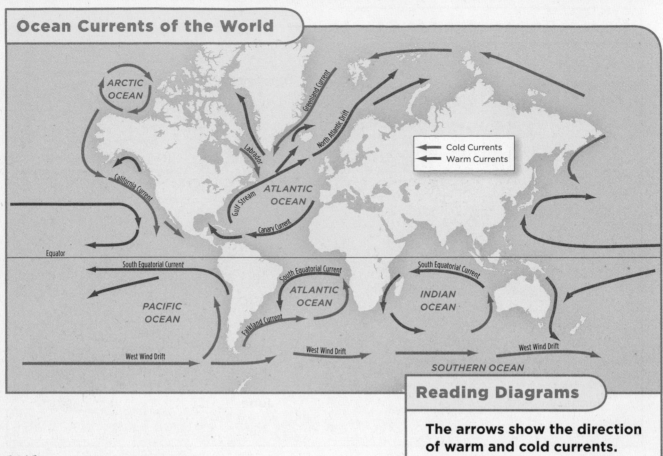

Ocean Currents of the World

ARCTIC OCEAN

Greenland Current

North Atlantic Drift

Labrador

California Current

Gulf Stream

ATLANTIC OCEAN

Canary Current

Equator

South Equatorial Current

South Equatorial Current

South Equatorial Current

PACIFIC OCEAN

ATLANTIC OCEAN

INDIAN OCEAN

Falkland Current

West Wind Drift

West Wind Drift

West Wind Drift

SOUTHERN OCEAN

Cold Currents
Warm Currents

Reading Diagrams

The arrows show the direction of warm and cold currents.

What are ocean currents?

A message in a bottle tossed into ocean off northern California would slowly drift south. It would be carried south by the California Current (KUR•uhnt). A **current** is an ongoing movement of ocean water.

The map shows cold and warm currents. For example, warm currents bring warm water from the equator toward the poles. Cold currents bring cold water from the poles toward the equator.

Warm currents heat up the air above the water. They warm up the land they pass by. Cold currents cool off the land they pass by.

✔ *Quick Check*

Label each as *cold* or *warm*.

17. California Current _____

18. Gulf Stream _____

What causes El Niño?

Usually there is a cold current along the Pacific Coast of Peru in South America. The air is cool and the air pressure is high. Winds blow toward Australia. There water is warmer and air pressure is lower.

However, every two to seven years, a change in the weather called *El Niño* happens. The cold current along Peru sinks. The surface water is warmer. So winds now blow toward the Americas. The winds push moist air, heavy rains, and storms onto the west coasts of North and South America.

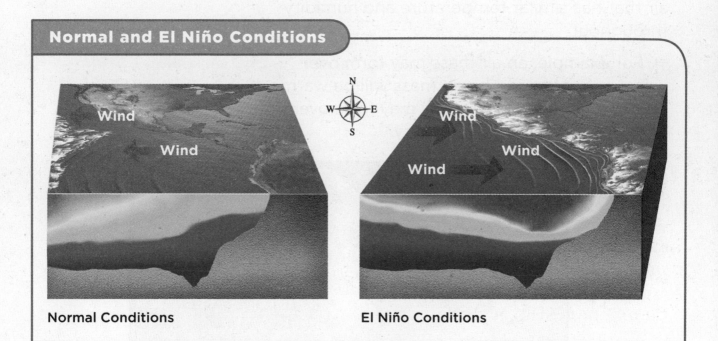

Normal and El Niño Conditions

Normal Conditions

El Niño Conditions

✓ Quick Check

19. In normal conditions the coast of Peru is cooled because _____

_____.

20. During El Niño storms affect the coasts of _____ and

_____.

LOG ON **e-Review** Summaries and quizzes online @ **www.macmillanmh.com**

What causes severe weather?

You may wake up to a warm, sunny day. However, as hours go by, the temperature may drop. Puffy clouds appear in the western sky. They soon are overhead and grow tall.

Why does weather change? Weather is affected by air masses that move across your area. An **air mass** is a large amount of air that has similar temperature and humidity throughout.

For example, an air mass may form over warm ocean water. The air mass will be warm and humid. Another air mass may form over cold land. It will be cool and dry.

▲ Towering clouds like these indicate that a storm is coming. It is sunny above the clouds but dark below.

Fronts

Weather changes when one air mass moves into another air mass. The meeting place between two air masses is called a **front**.

Warm Fronts A warm air mass moves over a cold air mass. Cirrus clouds form higher up and then stratus clouds form closer to the ground. There may be some light, steady rain or snow.

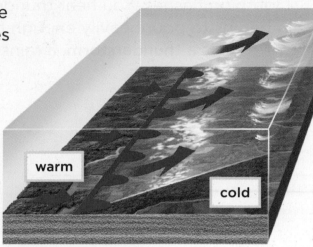

Warm Front: A warm air mass flows over a cold air mass.

Cold Fronts A cold air mass moves under a warm air mass. Warm air is pushed up along the front. Towering clouds may form and storms may break out.

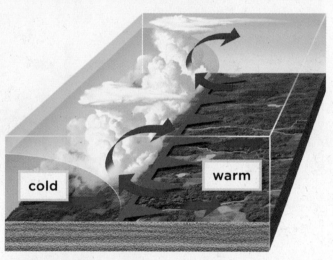

Cold Front: A cold air mass goes under a warm air mass.

✓ Quick Check

Fill in an effect of each cause below.

Cause	→	Effect
warm front →	**21.**	_____
cold front →	**22.**	_____

What causes thunderstorms?

Lightning flashes. You hear thunder nearby. Rain begins to pour heavily enough to flood a street. This is a **thunderstorm**, a rainstorm with thunder and lightning.

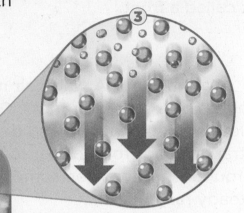

How a Thunderstorm Forms

① **cold front**

②

① **Fronts** A cold front moves in. Warm, humid air is pushed up. As it rises it expands and cools.

② **Thunderheads** The warm, humid air cools. Some of the water vapor condenses, forming water droplets. A cloud forms. Heat is released and surrounding air is warmed. This air rises even higher and forms a thunderhead.

③ **Precipitation** Water droplets combine and fall.

Reading Diagrams

What happens to the temperature of the air in a thundercloud?

LOG ON *Science in Motion* Watch how thunderstorms form @ **www.macmillanmh.com**

Lightning and Thunder

Have you ever shuffled your feet across a carpet? Shuffling or rubbing builds up static electricity in your body. You reach for a metal doorknob. A spark of electricity jumps from a finger to the doorknob.

Some scientists offer a similar explanation for lightning. Upward-moving wind (updrafts) push water up in a cloud. Gravity pulls water and ice down. Particles of water rub against particles going down. The rubbing builds up a charge of static electricity in the cloud. Lightning happens when the electricity jumps from the cloud.

Lightning heats the air around it. The heated air expands quickly, making the sound of thunder.

Thunderstorms can cause flooding, knock over trees, start fires, and hurt people.

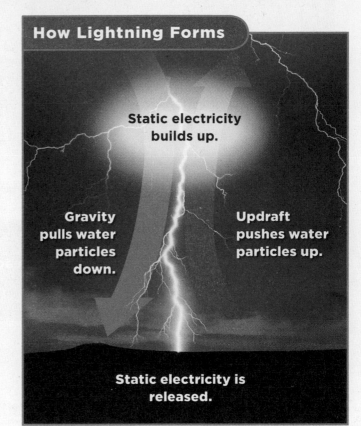

How Lightning Forms

Static electricity builds up.

Gravity pulls water particles down.

Updraft pushes water particles up.

Static electricity is released.

✔ Quick Check

For each number, circle what happens first.

23. A thundercloud forms.

A cold front moves in.

24. Static energy builds up in a cloud.

Water is pushed up and down inside a cloud.

25. Lightning jumps from a cloud.

Heated air makes the sound of thunder.

How a Tornado Forms

thunderhead

funnel cloud

① Warm air moves upward in a thunderhead.

② A funnel is formed when air starts spinning in the cloud.

What are tornadoes?

Under certain conditions, a thunderstorm can turn into a tornado (TAWR•nay•doh). A **tornado** is a spinning cloud shaped like a funnel, with winds up to 480 kilometers (299 miles) per hour.

The photos summarize how a tornado forms.

- **Warm air moves up in a thunderhead.** As warm air rises, air pressure inside the cloud becomes very low. This low pressure pulls in air from around the cloud.
- **Air flowing into the low pressure spins around in a circle.** As the air moves faster and faster, the cloud takes the shape of a funnel.
- **The tip of the funnel touches the ground.** It is now a tornado. That tip can carve through streets and buildings. Winds can lift and carry trees, cars, and pieces of homes.

tornado

3 The funnel cloud becomes a tornado when it touches the ground.

The numbers show the sequence of steps as a tornado forms.

Tornadoes can happen all over the United States. However, they are most common in Tornado Alley. This is a part of the country where cold, dry air from Canada meets warm, moist air from the Gulf of Mexico. This meeting can cause thunderstorms and tornadoes.

A tornado is an example of a cyclone (SIGH•klohn). A **cyclone** is a storm with low pressure at its center and spinning winds.

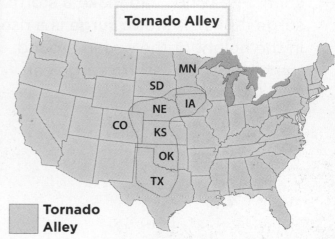

Tornado Alley

MN
SD
NE   IA
CO
KS
OK
TX

☐ Tornado
Alley

✔ **Quick Check**

Match the name and the description.
Fill in each blank with one of the following:

funnel cloud   thunderhead   tornado   cyclone

26. _____ a funnel cloud that touches the ground

27. _____ any spinning storm with low pressure

28. _____ a cloud that forms when air starts to spin

29. _____ a towering cloud that brings storms

What are hurricanes?

A thunderstorm over the Atlantic Ocean can become a *tropical storm*. A tropical storm has spinning winds with low pressure in the center. The low pressure pulls in water vapor from the ocean. It pulls in air from around the storm. The tropical storm can become a hurricane (HUR•i•kayn). A **hurricane** is a very large spinning storm with winds over 117 kilometers (73 miles) per hour.

A hurricane is a spiral of clouds with a hole, or *eye*, at its center. The fastest winds and heaviest rains are near the eye. The inside of the eye is calm. The winds can make a storm surge (SURJ). A **storm surge** is a rise in the height of the ocean around the hurricane. A storm surge can flood a coast.

Hurricane Katrina in August 2005 was one of the strongest hurricanes to reach the United States.

✔ Quick Check

30. How is a hurricane like a tornado? _____

_____

31. How is a hurricane different from a tornado? _____

_____

What are other forms of severe weather?

Heavy rain is severe weather. It can cause flooding if the rainwater cannot soak into the ground or drain away fast enough. Rain and flooding can cause landslides and mudslides.

A **monsoon** (mahn•SOON) in a seasonal wind that brings heavy rain. Monsoons happen in Southeast Asia. They also can happen in southwestern United States.

Fog can be severe weather if it is thick enough to limit vision beyond a fourth of a mile. Ground fog forms when warm air near the ground cools after sunset. Advection fog forms when warm air is pushed by wind over cool land or water.

monsoon

fog

✔ Quick Check

32. How can heavy rain be dangerous? _____

_____

33. How can fog be dangerous? _____

_____

Who needs to know what the weather will be?

You need to know what the weather will be so you can plan your day. So do people who work outdoors—builders, truck drivers, and letter carriers. Airplane pilots need to know the weather to make safe takeoffs and landings. Farmers must know the weather months ahead of time to plan crops to plant.

How can scientists forecast (FOR•kast) tomorrow's weather? To **forecast** means to "make a guess about what will happen based on what you know and see." For example, if you see something happen day after day, you may forecast that it will happen tomorrow.

Scientists use what they know and see to forecast the next day's weather. They know air pressure, wind speed and direction, air temperature, kinds of clouds, and so on.

▲ Air safety depends on knowing the weather ahead of time.

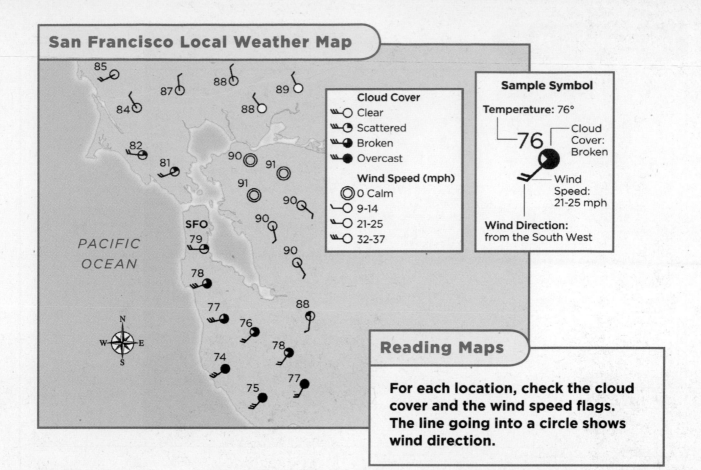

San Francisco Local Weather Map

Cloud Cover
- Clear
- Scattered
- Broken
- Overcast

Wind Speed (mph)
- 0 Calm
- 9-14
- 21-25
- 32-37

Sample Symbol

Temperature: 76°

76

Cloud Cover: Broken

Wind Speed: 21-25 mph

Wind Direction: from the South West

PACIFIC OCEAN

SFO

Reading Maps

For each location, check the cloud cover and the wind speed flags. The line going into a circle shows wind direction.

Weather Maps

A **weather map** shows the weather in a given area at one time. For each city or town, a weather map lists such information as:

- air temperature
- wind speed and direction
- cloud cover.

With this information each day for a week, you can forecast the next day's weather.

✔ Quick Check

34. Why is it important for bus and truck drivers to know the weather?

_____

_____

_____

35. What is the weather like at SFO (San Francisco Airport) on the weather map?

_____

_____

_____

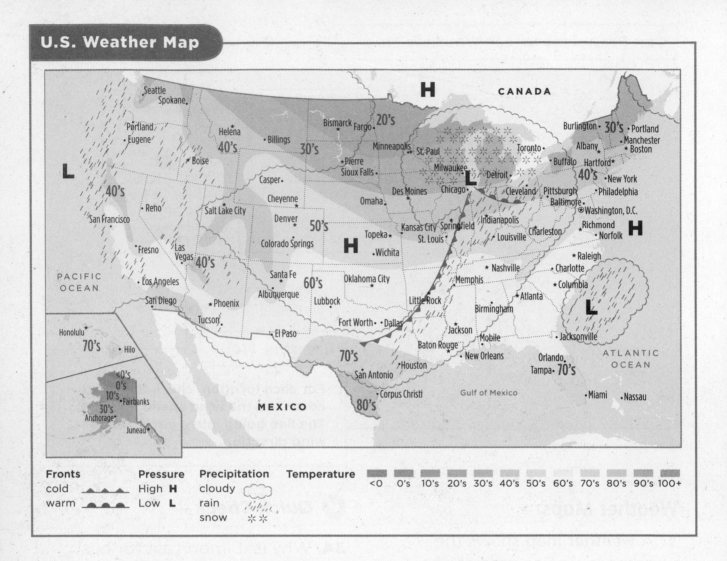

CANADA

Fronts
cold
warm

Pressure
High **H**
Low **L**

Precipitation
cloudy
rain
snow

Temperature
<0 | 0's | 10's | 20's | 30's | 40's | 50's | 60's | 70's | 80's | 90's | 100+

What do weather fronts tell you?

Weather maps of the United States often show warm fronts and cold fronts. A front is where one air mass is moving into another. Fronts drag cold or warm air along with them. You may find rain or a storm along a front.

Warm fronts are shown with red half circles. Cold fronts are shown with blue triangles. The circles and triangles point in the direction the fronts are moving.

Why are they moving? Global winds push air masses along. Global winds, remember, are winds that always blow in a given direction in a particular part of the world.

The West to East Rule

The jet stream is a global wind that blows across the United States. The jet stream blows high up in the sky, above mountains or buildings. Winds in the jet stream blow from west to east at speeds that can reach over 240 kilometers (150 miles) per hour.

Jet stream winds push air masses from west to east across the country. So on a weather map, find the weather in the west. If you know how fast the winds are blowing, you can tell how long it will take for the jet stream to blow that weather across the United States.

Front Moving from West to East

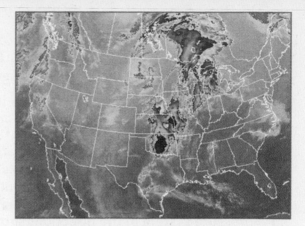

May 13, 2:00 p.m. Satellite image showing front over Canada.

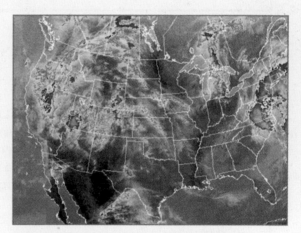

May 14, 2:00 p.m. Satellite image showing front over New York, Pennsylvania, and Virginia.

✓ Quick Check

36. What is the weather like in Indianapolis in the map? _____

_____

37. What may the weather be like in Indianapolis a day later? Explain.

_____

_____

What are lows and highs?

The map on page 122 labels parts of the country with L or H.

- L stands for a "low," a low pressure system.
- H stands for a "high," a high pressure system. Here is what lows and highs are like.

A Low Pressure System is a large mass of air with the lowest air pressure at the center.
- Winds blow in toward the center of a low pressure system in the directions shown by the arrows.
- Low pressure systems are warm and humid. They bring warm, stormy weather.

A High Pressure System is a large mass of air with the highest air pressure at the center.
- Winds blow out from the center of a high pressure system in the directions shown by the arrows.
- High pressure systems are cool and dry. They bring dry, clear, fair weather.

✓ Quick Check

How are highs and lows different?

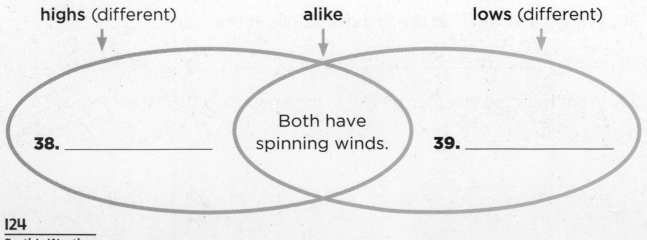

highs (different)   **alike**   **lows** (different)

38. _____   Both have spinning winds.   39. _____

Collecting Weather Information

Scientists collect weather data for the whole country and even around the world. They send weather satellites into space. They send up balloons into the atmosphere. The balloons have tools that measure air pressure, temperature, and humidity. They also use a device called Doppler radar to study storms. It can tell how a storm is moving.

They use these data to tell the weather over the next day or two.

Satellites take pictures of clouds and storms from space.

Weather balloons collect weather information from inside Earth's atmosphere.

✔ Quick Check

How are weather satellites and weather balloons different?

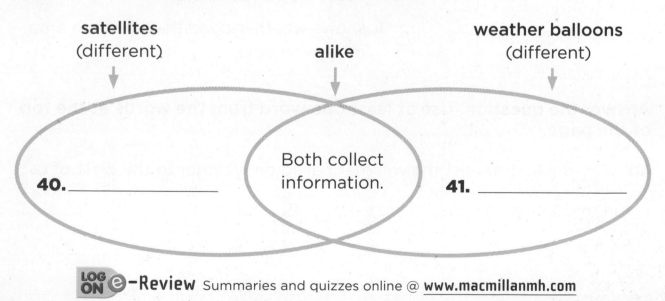

satellites
(different)

alike

weather balloons
(different)

40._____

Both collect information.

41._____

LOG ON e-Review Summaries and quizzes online @ **www.macmillanmh.com**

Earth's Weather

Match the descriptions with the words in the first column.

1. ___ air mass

2. ___ thunderstorm

3. ___ convection

4. ___ troposphere

5. ___ storm surge

6. ___ global wind

7. ___ air pressure

8. ___ weather map

9. ___ atmosphere

a. the layer of gases closest to Earth's surface

b. winds that blow around Earth in given directions over long distances

c. a rainstorm that includes lightning and thunder

d. heat going from one place to another through movement of a gas or liquid

e. air pressing onto a surface

f. a large amount of air that has similar temperature and humidity throughout

g. air that surrounds Earth

h. a large rise in the height of ocean water caused by a hurricane

i. shows weather conditions over an area at a given time

Answer the question. Use at least one word from the words at the top of the page.

10. Why do we forecast the weather based on weather to the west of us in the United States? _____

_____

_____

Write the missing words in the blanks. Then find the same words in the puzzle.

Across

1. water vapor in the air

2. the ongoing movement of ocean water

6. a tool that measures air pressure

7. the average weather conditions of a place

Down

1. a large spinning storm that has winds over 117 kilometers (73 miles) per hour

3. to make a guess about what may happen based on careful observation

4. a meeting place between two air masses

5. a spinning funnel cloud that has winds up to 480 kilometers (299 miles) per hour

7. any storm with low pressure at its center and spinning winds

CHAPTER 6

The Solar System

Vocabulary

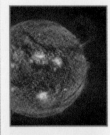
star an object in space that makes its own light and heat

astronomical unit the distance between Earth and the Sun

solar system the system of objects of, or around, the Sun

telescope a tool used to see distant objects

moon an object that circles around a planet

satellite any object in space that circles around another object

asteroid a rock that goes around the Sun

comet a mixture of frozen gases, ice, dust, and rock that moves in an irregular circle around the Sun

The Big Idea

What makes the planets move around the Sun?

meteor an object that crosses paths with Earth and enters Earth's atmosphere

gravity a pulling force between any two objects

orbit the path one object takes around another

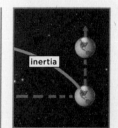

inertia the way objects act—a moving object keeps moving in a straight line unless it is pushed or pulled

ellipse a flattened circle

tide the daily rise and fall of the ocean's surface

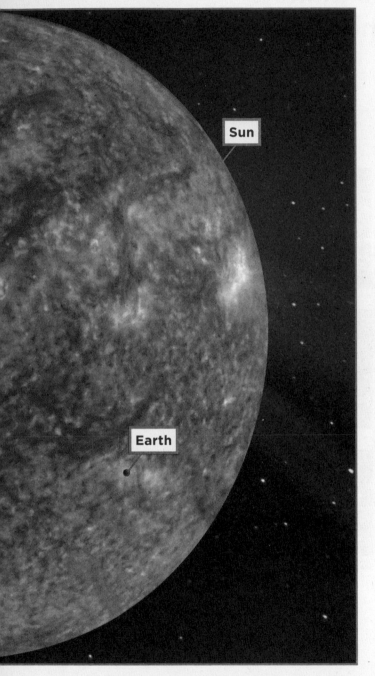

▲ If the Sun were a hollow ball, more than a million Earths could fit inside it.

What is the Sun?

The Sun is a star. A **star** is an object that produces its own energy. That energy includes heat and light. No other objects in space make their own energy.

The Sun is only an average-sized star. Many other stars are larger. They make millions of times more energy. Others stars are smaller and make less energy. However, the Sun is the only star in our solar system. It is the largest object in our solar system.

The Sun looks larger than other stars, because the Sun is much closer. The Sun is about 150 million kilometers (93 million miles) from Earth. The distance from Earth to the Sun is 1 AU, or **astronomical** (as•truh•NAH•mi•kuhl) **unit**. The closest other stars are about 270,000 AUs away from the solar system.

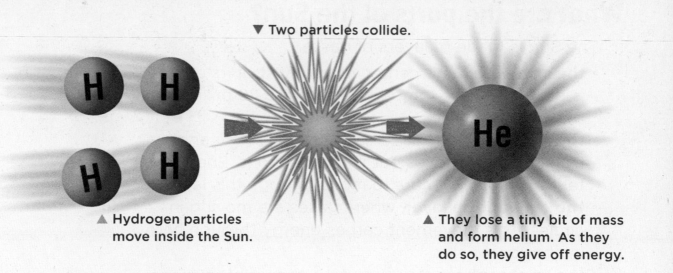

▼ Two particles collide.

▲ Hydrogen particles move inside the Sun.

▲ They lose a tiny bit of mass and form helium. As they do so, they give off energy.

The Sun's Mass

We cannot "weigh" the Sun. However, we can find out the Sun's mass, the amount of matter in the Sun. To do so, we need two facts:

- the time it takes a planet to go around the Sun (Earth takes 365.24 days)
- the distance of that planet to the Sun.

With these facts, we can tell the Sun's mass: 2 million trillion trillion kilograms. The Sun makes up 99.8% of the mass of our solar system.

The Sun is made up mostly of two gases. Hydrogen makes up most of the Sun (71%). Helium makes up 27%. Inside the Sun, particles of hydrogen are smashing together and giving off energy. See the diagram above.

✔ Quick Check

Match the word and the description.

1. ____ the Sun   **a.** distance from Earth to the Sun

2. ____ hydrogen   **b.** released when helium is made

3. ____ AU   **c.** most mass in the solar system

4. ____ energy   **d.** makes up most of the Sun

What are the parts of the Sun?

The Sun is made of layers of gases:

- **the core**, the Sun's center where most of its energy is produced. The temperature is 10 to 20 million degrees Celsius.
- **the radiation** (RAY•dee•a•shuhn) **layer**, where energy from the core moves out in all directions. Energy takes millions of years to move through this layer.
- **the convection layer**, where gases are moving in circles. This movement carries energy through here in about a week.
- **the photosphere** (FOH•tuh•sfeer), the visible surface of the Sun. The gases here are still very hot, but cooler than inside, about 6,000°C (10,000°F).

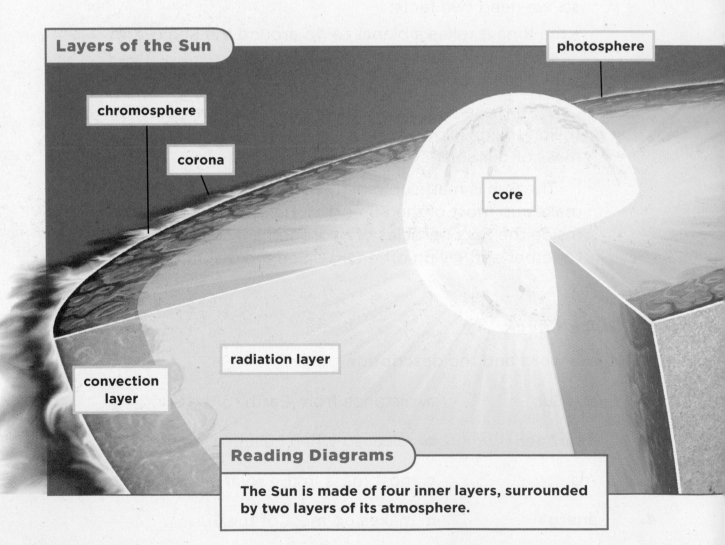

Layers of the Sun

chromosphere

corona

photosphere

core

radiation layer

convection layer

Reading Diagrams

The Sun is made of four inner layers, surrounded by two layers of its atmosphere.

The Sun's Atmosphere

Just outside the photosphere is the Sun's atmosphere. It is made of:

- **the chromosphere** (KROH•muh•sfeer), the inner layer of the Sun's atmosphere. When visible, it appears as a red circle around the Sun.
- **the corona** (kuh•ROH•nuh), the outer layer of the Sun's atmosphere. It takes on many shapes as inner temperatures change.

Bursts of energy called solar flares stretch from these two layers into space. Solar flares interrupt radios, cell phones, and TV.

Sunspots are dark spots in the photosphere. They appear dark because their temperatures are lower than the gases around them.

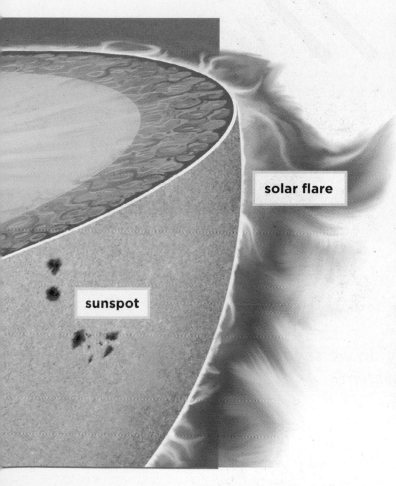

solar flare

sunspot

✔ Quick Check

Through which three layers does energy from the core move to get to the Sun's atmosphere?

5. First _____

⬇

6. Next _____

⬇

7. Last _____

8. Which part of the Sun do solar flares come from? _____

_____

What is the solar system?

The **solar system** is made up of the Sun and the objects that move around it.

Objects that move around the Sun include the eight planets and their moons. The planets are large ball-like bodies made up of rock and gases. The diagram on page 135 shows the eight planets in order from the Sun.

A **moon** is an object that circles a planet. Planets may have one or more moons—or no moons at all.

We see these objects with telescopes (TEL•uh•skohps). A **telescope** is a tool for seeing distant objects. We build telescopes on mountains and even send some into space to collect pictures. Space vehicles have explored all eight planets.

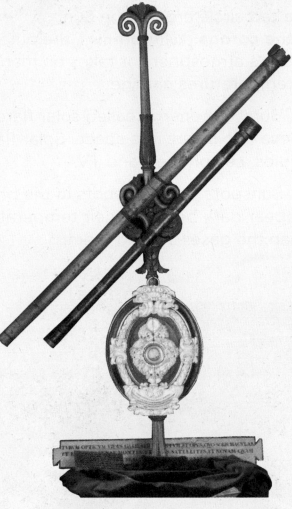

▲ The famous scientist Galileo Galilei used this telescope to view planets and moons in 1610.

✔ Quick Check

9. *Solar* means "of the Sun." Why do we say planets and their moons are parts of the *solar system*?

_____

_____

The Solar System

Planetary Data from NASA

Planet Name	Radius at the Equator (km)	Mean Surface Temperature (°C)	Surface Materials	Moons	Distance from Sun in A.U.
Mercury	2,440	179	Rock	0	0.39
Venus	6,052	482	Rock	0	0.7
Earth	6,378	15	Rock	1	1.0
Mars	3,397	-63	Rock	2	1.5
Jupiter	71,492	-121	Gas	at least 63	5.2
Saturn	60,268	-125	Gas	49	9.5
Uranus	25,559	-193	Gas	at least 27	19.2
Neptune	24,746	-193 to -153	Gas	13	30

✅ Quick Check

10. The largest planet is _____.

11. The planet with the hottest surface is _____.

12. The planet closet to Earth is _____.

Ganymede (Jupiter)

Moon (Earth)

Phobos (Mars)

Deimos (Mars)

1 cm
1,000 km

1 cm
10 km

▲ Two of the largest moons　　　　　▲ Two small moons

What is a moon?

Moons circle planets, but not all planets have them. Some planets have one moon or several moons, as you read in the table on page 135. Some moons are small. Others are large. Jupiter's Ganymede is the largest moon in the solar system.

Moons are natural satellites (SAT•uh•lights). A **satellite** is an object in space that circles another object. In addition, human-made satellites circle Earth. They are used for communication and to collect information about Earth.

Earth's Moon has many craters, or dents. They formed when other objects from space fell onto the surface. The Moon has no atmosphere. An atmosphere would cause small objects to burn up on the way down to the surface.

What are the smaller objects in the solar system?

In addition to planets and moons, other kinds of objects travel around the Sun.

- **asteroids** (AS•tuh•roids) There are thousands of **asteroids**, rocks that travel around the Sun. Most are between Mars and Jupiter. They can be from 1 mile to 500 miles wide.

- **comets** A **comet** is a mass of rock, frozen gases, ice, and dust. Comets have paths that approach the Sun. As a comet nears the Sun, a tail of gas and dust forms. The tail points away from the Sun and fades as the comet gets farther away from the Sun.

- **meteors** (MEE•tee•uhrs) **Meteors** are small objects from space that enter Earth's atmosphere.

A comet's tail points away from the Sun. Here the Sun is toward the upper left.

✔ Quick Check

Complete the diagram. Summarize the lesson.

planets and moons	asteroids	comets

13. Summary: _____

_____

_____

LOG ON e**-Review** Summaries and quizzes online @ **www.macmillanmh.com**

What is gravity?

Why do you fall when you trip? You fall because of the pull of gravity between you and Earth. **Gravity** is a pull between any two objects.

There is gravity throughout the solar system. For example, there is a pull of gravity between the Sun and each planet. The strength of gravity depends on:

• **distance** The closer two objects are to each other, the greater the pull is. The pull gets weaker when objects are farther apart.

• **mass** *Mass* means "how much matter" is in something. The greater the total mass of any two objects is, the stronger the pull of gravity is between the two objects.

Suppose you traveled from Earth to the Moon. Where is gravity stronger: on Earth or on the Moon?

The astronaut, John Young, could jump higher on the Moon than on Earth. Why? The pull of gravity is less on the Moon.

Gravity and Weight

Measuring your *weight* on a scale can help you compare gravity on Earth and the Moon. Your weight depends on two things:

- your mass (in kilograms)
- what the pull of gravity is where you are.

If you go to the Moon, your mass stays the same. However, Earth has more mass than the Moon. So the total mass of you and Earth is more than the total mass of you and the Moon. So gravity is stronger on Earth. You weigh more on Earth than on the Moon

The huge planet Jupiter has more mass than Earth. The pull of gravity on Jupiter is greater than on Earth. If you visited Jupiter, your mass would stay the same. However, you would weigh much more than on Earth.

Weight and Gravity

Mass = 100
Weight = 100 lbs

Mass = 100
Weight = 236 lbs

Mass = 100
Weight = 16.5 lbs

Earth
Gravity = 1

Jupiter
Gravity = 2.36

Moon
Gravity = 0.165

Note: Planets are not shown to scale.

Reading Diagrams

The boy's mass is always the same. His weight more than doubles on Jupiter. His weight on the Moon is only about $\frac{1}{6}$ his weight on Earth.

✓ Quick Check

Tell the "effect" on gravity for each "cause."

Cause	→	Effect
Two objects move closer together. →		**14.** _____
Two objects move father apart. →		**15.** _____

What keeps objects in orbit?

Planets travel around the Sun in almost circular paths. Moons travel around planets in similar kinds of paths. The path one object takes around another is called an **orbit**.

Objects are held in their orbits by gravity. For example, planets are held in their orbits around the Sun by the pull of gravity between each planet and the Sun.

The pull of gravity alone would pull a planet into the Sun. It takes gravity and inertia (in•UR•shuh) together to keep objects in their orbits. **Inertia** is a way in which objects act when they move or stay at rest. A moving object tends to keep moving in a straight line. An object at rest tends to stay at rest.

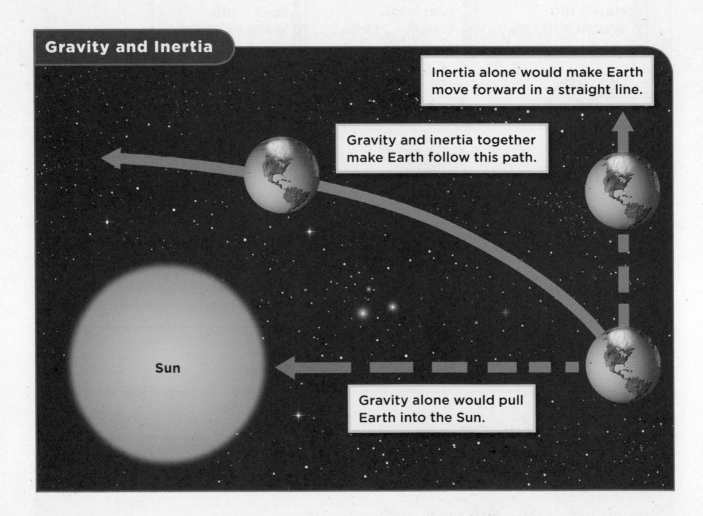

Gravity and Inertia

Inertia alone would make Earth move forward in a straight line.

Gravity and inertia together make Earth follow this path.

Sun

Gravity alone would pull Earth into the Sun.

Working Together

How do gravity and inertia work together? Think of a space vehicle orbiting Earth. Gravity is pulling the vehicle toward Earth. However, the vehicle and the crew don't feel this pull. The crew members are weightless.

Gravity is being balanced by the forward motion of the vehicle. In the same way, as planets orbit the Sun, gravity would pull them toward the Sun. However, the forward motion of the planets keeps them moving away from the Sun.

These two motions make planets move in nearly circular orbits. The shape of the orbit is an **ellipse**, a flattened circle. Because the orbit is not a perfect circle, Earth is farther from the Sun at certain times of the year than at other times.

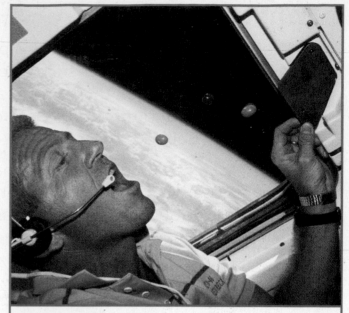

This astronaut catches weightless candy while in a space vehicle in orbit around Earth.

✔ Quick Check

Match the word and its description.

16. ____ ellipse   **a.** keeps an object moving forward

17. ____ inertia   **b.** the path of one object around another

18. ____ gravity   **c.** a flattened circle

19. ____ orbit   **d.** pulls planets toward the Sun

What causes tides?

You have learned that there is a pull of gravity between any two objects—such as between Earth and the Sun. However, there is also a pull of gravity between Earth and the Moon. Both of these pulls have an effect on Earth.

The Moon has much less mass than the Sun, but it is much closer to Earth. The pull between Earth and the Moon is about twice as strong as the pull between Earth and the Sun.

The pull is felt on Earth's oceans. This pull causes tides. A **tide** is a rise and fall of the ocean's surface.

Most oceans have two high tides and two low tides each 24-hour day. Earth spins on its axis all the time, making a complete spin in one day. As any point spins to face the Moon, ocean water bulges on that side and the opposite side (high tides). In between the bulges are the low tides.

high tide

low tide

Monthly Tides

Remember, the Moon is traveling in an orbit around earth. Twice a month, the Moon is in a point in its orbit directly in line with Earth and the Sun. See the new moon and full moon in the diagram.

At these two times, the pull of gravity of the Sun and of the Moon is in the same direction. This line up of Earth-Moon-Sun causes *spring tides*. In spring tides, high tides are higher than usual and low tides are lower than usual.

Twice each month, the Sun and the Moon are pulling in different directions. See the first and third quarter moons in the diagram. The pull of the Sun and of the Moon cancel each other out and cause neap tides. During neap tides the difference between a high tide and a low tide is smaller than any other time.

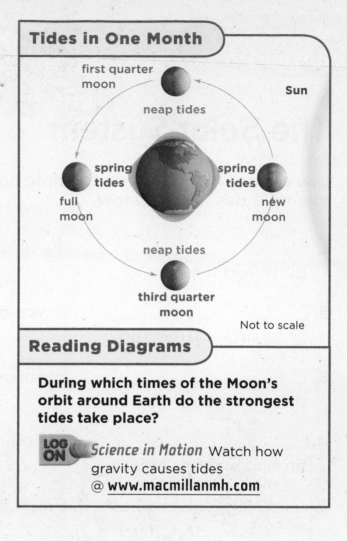

Tides in One Month

first quarter moon

Sun

neap tides

spring tides

spring tides

full moon

new moon

neap tides

third quarter moon

Not to scale

Reading Diagrams

During which times of the Moon's orbit around Earth do the strongest tides take place?

LOG ON *Science in Motion* Watch how gravity causes tides @ **www.macmillanmh.com**

✔ *Quick Check*

Cross out the term that does not belong in each row.

20. neap tides   full moon   third quarter moon

21. new moon   spring tides   first quarter moon

22. 24-hour day   two low tides   spring tides

LOG ON ℮-Review Summaries and quizzes online @ **www.macmillanmh.com**

The Solar System

Use a word from the box to name each
example described below.

asteroid
astronomical unit (Au)
gravity
inertia
satellite
solar system
telescope

1. _____ the distance between
Earth and the Sun

2. _____ a system of objects
of, or around, the Sun

3. _____ a tool used to see
distant objects

4. _____ any object in space that circles
around another object

5. _____ a rock that goes around the Sun

6. _____ the way objects act—a moving
object keeps moving in a straight line unless it is pushed
or pulled

7. _____ a pulling force between any
two objects

Use two words from the box to answer this question.

8. What are two things that work together keeping planets
in their orbits around the Sun?

_____

_____

_____

Fill in the following blanks with words from the box. Then find each word in the puzzle.

comet
ellipse
meteor
moon
orbit
star
tide

1. _____ an object in space that makes its own light and heat

2. _____ an object that circles around a planet

3. _____ a mixture of frozen gases, ice, dust, and rock that moves in an irregular circle around the Sun

4. _____ an object that crosses paths with Earth and enters Earth's atmosphere

5. _____ the path one object takes around another

6. _____ the rise and fall of the ocean's surface

7. _____ a flattened circle

```
Q W V S D E X A L
C O M E T H Q M O
M R C K F A V E T
X B K J G N R T S
P I R Y M P A E M
L T I D E Z T O D
E L L I P S E R B
D Q M O O N T S C
W N C A H S U P J
```

CHAPTER 7

Types of Matter

Vocabulary

 **volume** the space an object takes up

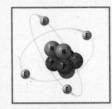 **atom** the smallest particle of an element that has all the properties of an element

 **mass** the amount of matter in an object

 **molecule** a particle that contains more than one atom joined together

 **matter** anything that has mass and volume

 **metal** a substance that conducts heat and electricity well

 **density** a measure of how tightly matter is packed in an object

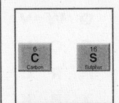 **nonmetal** an element that is a poor conductor of heat and electricity

 **element** the simplest kind of substance there is

 **metalloid** one of a group of elements that have properties of metals and nonmetals

What do all types of matter have in common?

 periodic table a table that arranges all known elements in rows and columns based on their properties

 **mixture** a combination of two or more substances that keep their properties

 **suspension** a mixture in which the particles settle and separate over time

 **solution** a mixture that stays mixed and you can see through clearly

 **solvent** the part of a solution that does the dissolving

solute the part of a solution that gets dissolved

 **filtering** a way of separating particles of different sizes

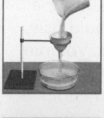 **chemical change** a change in matter that produces a new substance with new properties

 **compound** a substance formed when two or more other substances are combined and a chemical change takes place

 **hydrocarbons** compounds made of hydrogen and carbon

What is matter?

Put it on a balance and the pan goes down. Drop it into a cylinder of water. The water level goes up. What is it? The answer is matter.

Matter can be a solid, liquid, or gas. Matter takes up space. The amount of space it takes up is its **volume** (VOL•yewm).

To find the volume of a liquid, pour it into a clinder like the one shown here. Drop a solid into the liquid. The amount the liquid rises is the volume of the solid. Volume is measured in milliliters (mL) for liquids and gases, and cubic centimeters (cc or cm³) for solids.

The amount of matter in any object is its **mass**. To find the mass, put an object on a balance. Mass is measured in grams (g).

In summary, **matter** is anything that has mass and volume.

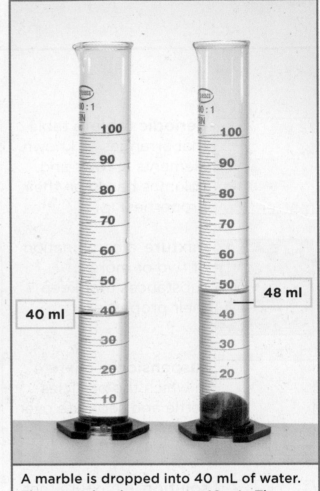

40 ml

48 ml

A marble is dropped into 40 mL of water. The water level goes up to 48 mL. The volume of the ball is 48-40, or 8 mL.

✔ Quick Check

Match the word with the description.

1. _____ volume   **a.** any solid, liquid, or gas

2. _____ mass   **b.** the space something takes up

3. _____ matter   **c.** the measurement taken with a balance

Mass and Weight

When you step on a spring scale, you measure your weight. Weight is a measure of how strongly gravity pulls on an object. It is measured in newtons (N) or pounds (lb).

Weight can change. It depends on the pull of gravity on an object. On other planets, gravity is weaker or stronger than on Earth. So an object's weight would be less or more than on Earth.

Weight is not the same as mass. Mass is the amount of matter in an object. It is measured with a balance. It always stays the same, no matter where the object is.

Volume, mass, and weight are all ways of describing matter. These are some properties of matter.

The mass of the marble is measured with a pan balance. It is always the same.

✔ Quick Check

Fill in each blank with *goes up* or *goes down*.

4. You drop a pebble into a cylinder of water. The water level

_____.

5. You place a pebble on a pan of a balance. The pan

_____.

6. Gravity is weaker on the Moon than on Earth. So on the

Moon, your weight _____.

What are states of matter?

Matter includes all solids, liquids, and gases.

Solid, liquid, and gas are the three states of matter. They are the forms matter can take.

- **solids** Particles that make up a solid are packed together tightly. They hardly move, except to "wiggle" in place. So the shape or volume (size) does not change.

- **liquids** Particles that make up a liquid can move past each other but stay close. So the shape of a liquid changes with the container it is in. However, the volume does not change.

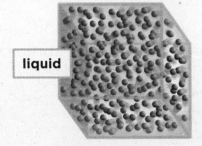

- **gases** Particles that make up a gas move around freely and can spread apart. So both the shape *and* the volume of a gas change to fit the container the gas is in.

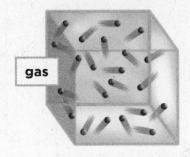

✔ Quick Check

Match the state with the description.

7. ____ solid   **a.** The volume changes.

8. ____ liquid   **b.** The shape stays the same.

9. ____ gas   **c.** Particles move but stay close.

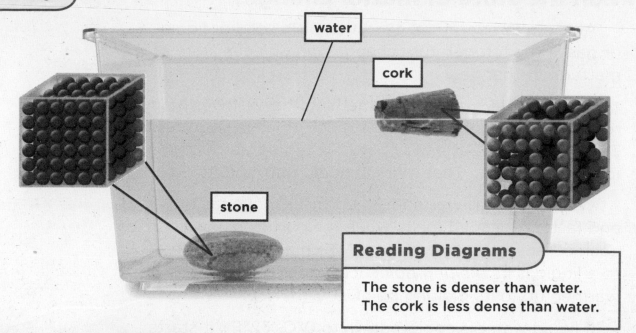

water

cork

stone

Reading Diagrams

The stone is denser than water.
The cork is less dense than water.

What is density?

Both the stone and the cork in the picture are solids. So why does the stone sink and the cork float? The particles that make up the stone are tightly packed. The particles that make up the cork are less tightly packed.

The rock has a greater density (DEN•si•tee) than the cork. **Density** is a measure of how tightly matter is packed in an object.

The stone and the cork have about the same size (volume). However, the denser stone has more mass—because it has more particles packed into its volume.

An object sinks in a liquid if it is denser than the liquid. The stone is denser than water. An object floats in a liquid if it is less dense than the liquid. The cork is less dense than water.

✔ Quick Check

Write *greater* or *lesser* in each blank.

10. Water has a _____ density than the stone.

11. The stone has a _____ density than the water.

Can the state of matter change?

At room temperature, everything is a solid or liquid or gas. If the temperature changes, an object's state of matter can change.

For example, start with something that is lower than room temperature—ice. Hold a piece of ice in your hand. The warmth of your hand raises the temperature of the ice. The ice *melts*. That is, it changes from solid to liquid.

When a solid is warmed, its particles move faster and faster. The solid melts when the particles flow past each other. The temperature at which a solid changes to a liquid is its *melting point*. Ice starts to melt if it is warmed up to its melting point, 0°C (32°F).

If liquid water is cooled down to 0°C (32°F), it starts to freeze. The temperature at which something freezes is its *freezing point*.

Ice melts at 0°C (32°F).

Liquid water freezes at 0°C (32°F).

Boiling

If you left a bowl of water uncovered in sunlight, evaporation (i•VAP•purh•ray•shuhn) would take place. During evaporation, warmed particles from the liquid slowly escape into the air. The liquid becomes a gas. Water in the form of gas is water vapor.

If you boil water, the particles of water escape into the air *quickly*. The boiling point is the temperature at which a liquid changes *quickly* to a gas. Water boils at 100°C (212°F).

When water vapor cools, the particles slow down and come closer together again. The gas changes into a liquid. The temperature at which a gas changes to a liquid is the *condensing point*. Some solids change directly to a liquid with melting.

Water boils at 100°C (212°F).

Water vapor condenses at 100°C (212°F).

✔ *Quick Check*

Fill in two details to explain the main idea.

Main Idea	Details
Matter can change state.	12. _____ _____ 13. _____

LOG ON ℮-Review Summaries and quizzes online @ www.macmillanmh.com

What is an element?

Centuries ago, the ancient Greeks thought that all kinds of matter were made of four simple substances. They identified air, fire, earth, and water as the building blocks of all matter.

Today, we know of over 100 building blocks of matter, the elements. An **element** is the simplest kind of substance, something that cannot be broken into anything simpler. These elements are the substances that are combined in all kinds of matter.

Some of the commonly known elements are:

- gases—oxygen, nitrogen, hydrogen
- liquids (only two)—bromine, mercury
- solids (the most)—carbon, aluminum, iron, copper, sulfur, nickel, siver, gold

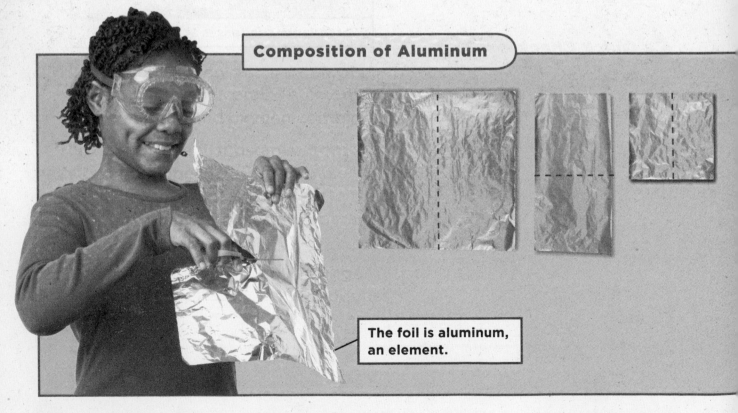

Composition of Aluminum

The foil is aluminum, an element.

Names, Symbols, Atoms

The names of elements come from many places. The element mercury was named after a character from ancient Roman myths. The element californium was named for our state.

Each element has a symbol for its name. A symbol is made of:
- one capital letter, such as O for oxygen, OR
- a capital letter followed by a small letter, such as Zn for zinc.

Symbols come from many languages—such as Latin and Greek. For example, Au, for gold, is from the Latin word for gold, *aurum*.

Each element is made up of tiny particles called atoms (A•tuhmz). An **atom** is the smallest particle that makes up an element and has the properties of that element. To get an atom, you would have to keep breaking a piece of an element into smaller and smaller bits.

✔ Quick Check

Match the word with the description.

14. ____ element   **a.** a letter or two to stand for a name

15. ____ atom   **b.** the simplest kind of substance

16. ____ symbol   **c.** the smallest kind of particle

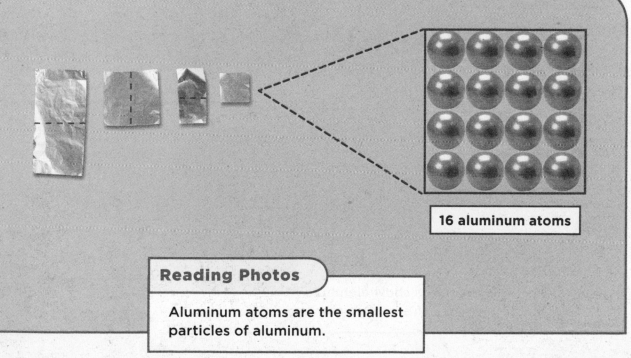

16 aluminum atoms

Reading Photos

Aluminum atoms are the smallest particles of aluminum.

What are the most common elements?

Of the over 100 known elements, 92 were found in nature. The others were made by scientists in laboratories. Only eight elements make up about 98% (by weight) of Earth's surface layer, the crust. Two elements, oxygen and silicon, head the list. The rest of the natural elements are in the crust as well, but in very small amounts.

The oceans are made largely of two elements, oxygen and hydrogen, 96% by weight. Chlorine and sodium from salt make up 3%.

Just two elements, nitrogen and oxygen, make up 99% of Earth's air. Most of the air is nitrogen, but we must breathe in oxygen. A few other elements make up 15% of the air.

✔ Quick Check

17. Which element is common in the air, water, *and* the crust?

_____

_____

Composition of Earth

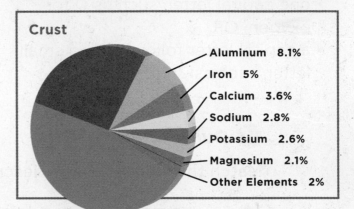

Crust

Aluminum 8.1%
Iron 5%
Calcium 3.6%
Sodium 2.8%
Potassium 2.6%
Magnesium 2.1%
Other Elements 2%

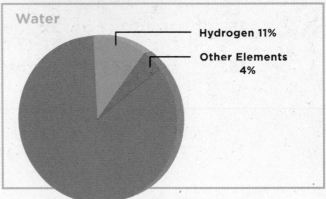

Water

Hydrogen 11%
Other Elements 4%

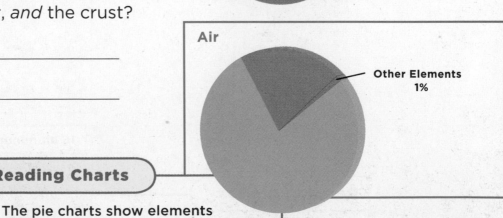

Air

Other Elements 1%

Reading Charts

The pie charts show elements found in Earth's crust, water and air.

Elements in Living Things

Plants have thick cell walls and other parts for support. These parts are made mainly of the elements carbon, hydrogen, and oxygen.

Animals, too, are made mainly of the elements carbon, hydrogen, and oxygen. The bodies of animals contain a great deal of water. Human body weight is over 60% water. Much of the oxygen and hydrogen in our bodies is from the water we contain.

Bones, teeth, and other parts also contain nitrogen, phosphorus, and some chlorine and sulfur.

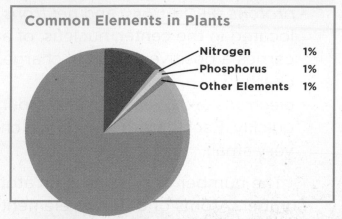

Common Elements in Plants

Nitrogen	1%
Phosphorus	1%
Other Elements	1%

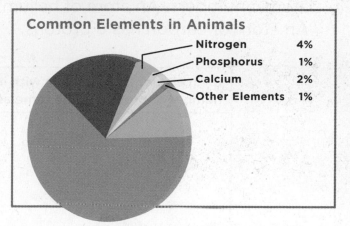

Common Elements in Animals

Nitrogen	4%
Phosphorus	1%
Calcium	2%
Other Elements	1%

✔ Quick Check

18. Circle the row that has the three most common elements in living things, listed from the most to the least:

nitrogen	oxygen	carbon
oxygen	carbon	hydrogen
mercury	calcium	oxygen

LOG ON ℮ –**Review** Summaries and quizzes online @ **www.macmillanmh.com**

What are atoms and molecules?

Remember, if you split an element into smaller and smaller pieces, you eventually get an atom of the element. If you could split an atom, you would see the pieces the atom is made of.

- *protons* (PROH•tahns) and *neutrons* (NEW•trons) are located in the center, nucleus, of an atom. Each proton carries a positive electrical charge. Neutrons are not charged.
- *electrons* (e•LEK•trahns) move around the nucleus very quickly. Each carries a negative charge. Electrons are very small.

The number of protons in an atom is the atomic number. Atoms of different elements have different atomic numbers. An atom of helium has only 2 protons. An atom of carbon has 6 protons.

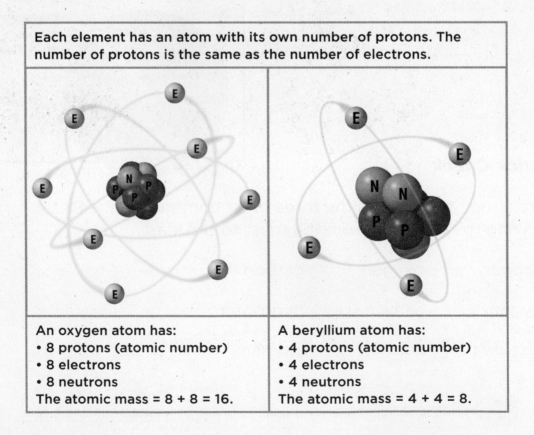

Each element has an atom with its own number of protons. The number of protons is the same as the number of electrons.

An oxygen atom has:
- 8 protons (atomic number)
- 8 electrons
- 8 neutrons
The atomic mass = 8 + 8 = 16.

A beryllium atom has:
- 4 protons (atomic number)
- 4 electrons
- 4 neutrons
The atomic mass = 4 + 4 = 8.

Atoms of each element have their own atomic mass. The atomic mass is the sum of the protons and neutrons of an atom. Electrons are not counted because they have so little mass.

Atoms of some elements are found naturally as molecules (MOL•uh•kyewls). A **molecule** is a particle made of more than one atom joined together. For example, oxygen exists as molecules. A molecule of oxygen is made of 2 oxygen atoms joined together. The symbol for an oxygen molecule is O_2.

Molecules can be made of atoms of different elements. For example, water molecules are made of 2 hydrogen atoms and 1 oxygen atom.

Symbol: O_2

An oxygen molecule is made of 2 oxygen atoms that are joined together.

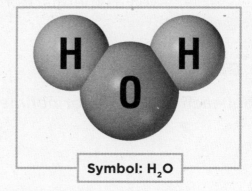

Symbol: H_2O

A water molecule is made of 1 oxygen atom and 2 hydrogen atoms joined together.

✔ Quick Check

Cross out the word or term in each row that does not belong. Explain your answer.

19. proton   neutron   electron   molecule

_____

_____

20. atomic mass   protons   neutrons   electrons

_____

_____

What are properties of elements?

Many elements have similar properties.

- Most elements are metals. **Metals** conduct heat and electricity well. They can be bent or flattened without breaking. They are usually solids at room temperature. Examples are: aluminum, gold, iron, copper, and silver.
- There are 17 nonmetals. **Nonmetals** do not conduct heat and electricity well. Solid nonmetals, like carbon, break rather than bend. Most nonmetals are gases, like helium, oxygen, and nitrogen. Bromine is a liquid.
- A small group of elements called **metalloids** (MET•uh•loids) conduct heat and electricity, but not as well as metals. Boron and silicon are metalloids.

✔ Quick Check

Label each as a *metal* or *nonmetal*.

21. _____

22. _____

23. _____

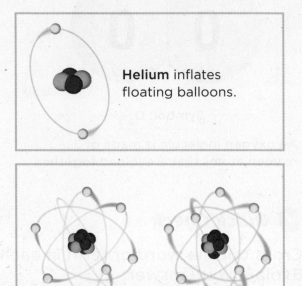

Helium inflates floating balloons.

Nitrogen/Oxygen make up 98 percent of air.

Iron in the fence is strong and heavy.

Can we see atoms?

In a pinch of salt there are over a half billion sodium atoms and a half billion chlorine atoms. That's how small atoms are. We can't see them with just our eyes. However, we can see them with special microscopes.

- The electron microscope, invented in 1932, hits atoms with a beam of electrons. It allowed us to see molecules.

- The field ion microscope, invented in 1951, bounces electrically charged particles called ions (EYE•ahns) on atoms. It allowed us to see molecules and large atoms.

- The modern scanning tunneling microscope uses a very fine tip to grab atoms or groups of atoms. The tip can then drag them on a surface.

- The very new one-angstrom microscope shows the atoms lined up inside a metal.

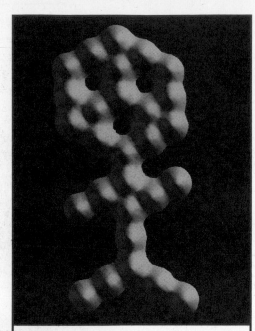

With a tunneling microscope, 28 two-atom groups were moved onto a platinum surface in a shape called Molecule Man.

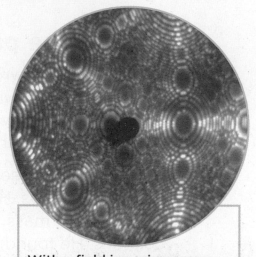

With a field ion microscope, atoms appear as bright spots.

✔ Quick Check

24. Circle the microscope that is out of order.

electron   scanning tunneling   field ion   one-angstrom

25. Why are these special microscopes important? _____

_____

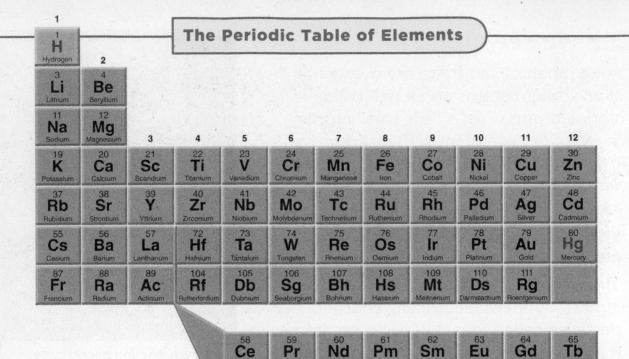

What is the periodic table?

Suppose you wrote out the name of each element on a card. Along with the name, you list properties of each element. How would you organize your cards to show which elements are alike?

Dmitri Mendeleev (DMEE•tree men•DEL•ee•ef) did just that in the 1800s. He organized the cards in order of increasing mass. He laid them out into rows and columns. He found that all the elements in any column have similar properties.

Mendeleev organized the periodic (peer•ee•OD•ik) table. The **periodic table** is a chart with the elements in rows and columns of increasing atomic number. You see the atomic number in each box in the table. As you go from row to row, the properties repeat themselves (periodic refers to "repeating").

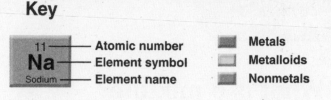

Key

Na — Atomic number, Element symbol, Element name (Sodium, 11)	Metals	
	Metalloids	
	Nonmetals	

State at Room Temperature:

Black: solid

Purple: liquid

Red: gas

> ### Reading Tables
>
> The key helps you find information about elements on the periodic table.

Periodic table (columns 13–18):

13	14	15	16	17	18
					2 **He** Helium
5 **B** Boron	6 **C** Carbon	7 **N** Nitrogen	8 **O** Oxygen	9 **F** Fluorine	10 **Ne** Neon
13 **Al** Aluminum	14 **Si** Silicon	15 **P** Phosphorus	16 **S** Sulphur	17 **Cl** Chlorine	18 **Ar** Argon
31 **Ga** Gallium	32 **Ge** Germanium	33 **As** Arsenic	34 **Se** Selenium	35 **Br** Bromine	36 **Kr** Krypton
49 **In** Indium	50 **Sn** Tin	51 **Sb** Antimony	52 **Te** Tellurium	53 **I** Iodine	54 **Xe** Xenon
81 **Tl** Thallium	82 **Pb** Lead	83 **Bi** Bismuth	84 **Po** Polonium	85 **At** Astatine	86 **Rn** Radon

66 **Dy** Dysprosium	67 **Ho** Holmium	68 **Er** Erbium	69 **Tm** Thulium	70 **Yb** Ytterbium	71 **Lu** Lutetium
98 **Cf** Californium	99 **Es** Einsteinium	100 **Fm** Fermium	101 **Md** Mendelevium	102 **No** Nobelium	103 **Lr** Lawrencium

Similar Elements

When the elements are listed by increasing atomic number in rows of no more than 18,

- all the metals are together (blue boxes)
- all the nonmetals are together (green boxes)
- all the metalloids are together (yellow boxes)
- all the gases are together (symbols in red)

The columns have groups or families of elements, elements with similar properties. For example, column number 17 has all the *halogen* (HAL•uh•jen) gases. These gases have a foul smell. They can burn flesh and combine with metals. Column 18 has the noble gases. These gases are "inactive" elements. They don't combine with other elements.

✓ Quick Check

26. How many gases are there? How can you tell?

_____

_____

_____

27. How many metalloids are there? How can you tell?

_____

_____

_____

LOG ON e-Review Summaries and quizzes online @ **www.macmillanmh.com**

What is a mixture?

Trail mix is a tasty mixture (MIKS•chuhr). A **mixture** is a combination of two or more things that keep their own properties. You can pick apart the things that make up trail mix—such as nuts and pretzels. Each item keeps its taste and shape.

Trail mix is a mixture in which the particles inside are big enough to see. Tossed salad is another example. These mixtures do not look the same throughout. There may be more nuts in one part and more pretzels in another.

In other mixtures, the particles that are mixed together are too small to see. Milk is an example. You cannot see the particles inside.

Concrete is a solid mixture. It is made up of small pieces of rocks, fine sand, fine cement powder, and water. The parts are thoroughly mixed into a pourable mud that hardens into a strong material that does not settle out.

The CN Tower in Toronto, Canada, is made from a solid mixture, concrete.

◀ Trail mix is a mixture of many kinds of tasty snacks in one.

To Settle or Not to Settle

The particles in some mixtures settle out. In others, the particles do not settle out. A **suspension** (suh•SPEN•shuhn) is a mixture in which the particles settle and separate into layers over time. For example, shake oil and vinegar to make a smooth suspension. Then let it sit. In time the oil layers out on top of the vinegar.

The particles in some mixtures are the size of atoms or molecules. These mixtures are solutions (suh•LEW•shuhns). A **solution** is a mixture that stays mixed because its particles are as small as atoms or molecules.

You make a solution by dissolving one substance in another, like sugar in water. Solutions are the same throughout. If they are liquid or gas, you can see through them clearly.

A suspension of oil and vinegar separates into its parts when it stands still.

Window cleaner is a solution. It stays mixed. You can see through it.

✔ *Quick Check*

28. You shake oil and water together. How can you tell if you

have made a suspension or a solution? _____

_____

29. Circle the word that includes the other two:

mixture   solution   suspension

What are the parts of a solution?

Add sugar to water and stir. The sugar *dissolves*. That is, it breaks into particles the size of molecules and seems to disappear in the water. However, the sugar is still there because the mixture is sweet.

All solutions have a part that dissolves another part. The **solvent** (SOL•vuhnt) is the part that does the dissolving, such as water. The part that gets dissolved, such as sugar, is the **solute** (SOL•yewt).

The solute or the solvent can be a solid, a liquid, or a gas. The solvent is usually the part there is more of. For example, air is a mixture of gases. Most of the air is nitrogen. Nitrogen is the solvent. Other gases, like oxygen, are the solutes dissolved in the nitrogen.

solute

solvent

solution

Reaching a Limit

Have you ever tried stirring table salt into water? At first the salt dissolves. However, as you add more, the added salt falls to the bottom, no matter how hard you stir.

A solvent (water) can dissolve only a certain amount of solute (salt). At room temperature, only 37 grams of table salt dissolves into 100 grams of water. Extra salt does not dissolve.

Is there a way to get the extra salt to dissolve? One way is to use warm water. Heating water can allow more solid solute to dissolve.

There is a limit to how much solute can disolve. When the limit is reached, the extra solute falls to the bottom.

However, heating can have the opposite effect when the solute is a gas. For example, seltzer is a solution of a gas (carbon dioxide) and water. Cool seltzer holds more carbon dioxide gas than warm seltzer.

✔ Quick Check

30. Circle the word that includes the other two:

solute   solution   solvent

31. What effect can heating have on a solution? _____

_____

▲ Sand and water: Sand particles cannot pass through the holes in the filter. Water goes through, but sand collects on the filter.

▲ Sawdust and sand in water: Let the mixture stand still. Sawdust floats to the top and sand collects on the bottom.

How can you take mixtures apart?

Make three mixtures: sand in water, sawdust and sand in water, sugar and sand in water. Can you get the solids back? Mixtures are *physical combinations*. That means their properties do not change. So you should be able to separate the solids from the liquid.

- One way to separate them is by filtering (FIL•ter•ing). **Filtering** separates substances that have particles of different sizes. Pour the mixture over a filter. A filter has small holes. Small particles pass with the liquid through the holes. Larger particles are trapped by the filter.

- If substances have different densities, some may float or sink in water. For example, sand is denser than water. It sinks when the mixture is kept still. Sawdust is less dense than water. It floats to the top.

▲ Sugar and sand in water: Sand falls to the bottom. Pour the liquid through a filter. Let the water evaporate. The sugar remains behind.

▲ Iron and sand in water: A magnet attracts the iron filings, but not the sand.

- If you have a solid solute (like sugar) dissolved in water, just let the solution stand open to the air for several days. The water evaporates and leaves the solid solute behind.
- Suppose you spilled iron filings into sand. You can separate the iron by using a magnet. The magnet attracts iron, while the sand remains behind.

Reading Diagrams

How would you separate a mixture of sand, sawdust, sugar, and iron filings in water?

LOG ON *Science in Motion* Watch how mixtures are separated @ **www.macmillanmh.com**

✔ Quick Check

Match each solid with a way of separating it from water.

32. ____ sawdust   **a.** evaporating

33. ____ sand   **b.** using a magnet

34. ____ sugar   **c.** floating

35. ____ iron filings   **d.** sinking

LOG ON ℮-**Review** Summaries and quizzes online @ **www.macmillanmh.com**

Iron in this ship combined with oxygen in the air and formed rust, a brownish material that crumbles.

What changes produce new and different substances?

Have you ever seen rust on a bicycle fender or a car? Rust forms when iron comes into contact with oxygen, a gas in the air. Iron and oxygen combine and form rust.

Rust is a different substance from iron or oxygen, with its own properties. For example, rust has a different color than iron. You cannot separate the iron and oxygen from rust as simply as you can separate parts of a mixture.

Rust forms from a chemical change. A **chemical change** is change in matter that produces substances different from the substances you started with. To separate the iron from the oxygen would take another chemical change.

Compounds

Rust forms when atoms of iron combine with atoms of oxygen. Rust is an example of a compound (KAHM•pownd). A **compound** is formed when atoms of two or more elements are combined. The chemical name of rust is iron oxide. The name shows that rust is made of iron and oxygen.

Sugar is another example of a compound. Sugar molecules are made of atoms of three elements: carbon, hydrogen, and oxygen.

A marshmallow is white sugar. What happens when a marshmallow is toasted? There is a chemical change. In this change, heat moves about the atoms in the sugar to produce a black material, the carbon, and steam. Steam is water, a compound of hydrogen and oxygen.

Chemical Changes

Reading Photos

The marshmallows, sugar, are changing chemically. The burning sticks are also changing chemically. Both are producing a black substance, carbon.

✅ *Quick Check*

Write *true* or *false*. If it is false, explain why.

36. A chemical change produces new substances. _____

_____

37. A compound is a kind of mixture. _____

_____

How are compounds named?

What we call rust is a compound made from two elements—iron and oxygen. The chemical name of rust is iron oxide. The name comes from one element (iron) plus a changed form of the other element (oxygen ⟶ oxide).

iron + oxygen ⟶ iron oxide (rust)

Another example is table salt. It is a compound made of the metal element sodium and the gaseous element chlorine. The chemical name of salt uses both the element names:

sodium + chlorine ⟶ sodium chloride (table salt)

Compounds can also be written in a short way called a *chemical formula* (FOR•myew•luh). A chemical formula uses symbols and sometimes numbers. For example, water is a compound of hydrogen (H) and oxygen (O). We can use symbols to write it as:

Water: H_2O

The small 2 placed after the H means that a molecule of water is made of 2 atoms of hydrogen combined with an oxygen atom.

Mon & Di

Sometimes we add prefixes to a chemical name to help tell one compound from another. For example, carbon and oxygen can combine in two ways. One atom of carbon can combine with one atom of oxygen: We put the prefix *mon* with the oxygen to show one oxygen atom:

CO (carbon *mon*oxide) is made of 1 C atom + 1 O atom.

Carbon monoxide is the dangerous gas that you must watch out for at home.

A carbon atom can also combine with two oxygen atoms. That forms carbon dioxide (*di* means "two," as in 2 oxygen atoms). Carbon dioxide is a gas that you release when you exhale. It is also present in smoke.

Carbon dioxide: CO$_2$

CO$_2$ (carbon *di*oxide) is made of 1 C atom + 2 O atoms.

✓ Quick Check

Here is a molecule of sugar. Some of the hydrogen atoms are not visible behind the other atoms.

Sugar: C$_6$H$_{12}$O$_6$

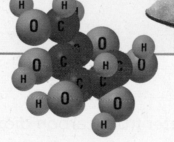

Tell how many of each atom are in one molecule of sugar.

38. ____ carbon atoms

39. ____ hydrogen atoms

40. ____ oxygen atoms

How can you identify compounds?

There are millions of compounds all around. Each one has its own properties. Some properties include: density, color, and freezing, melting, and boiling points. How a compound changes chemically is also a property.

You can use these properties to tell one compound from another. For example:

water	carbon dioxide
clear *liquid* at room temperature	colorless *gas* at room temperature
freezes at 0°C (32°F) boils at 100°C (212°F)	changes from gas directly to solid at –78°C (–108°F)
density = 1 gram per mL	1.5 times denser than air
puts out a flame	puts out a flame

You can tell what is in some compounds by the color a compound makes when it is held in a flame. Special computers are used today to heat compounds until they give off colors. The colors show what elements are in the compounds.

Compounds that contain potassium have violet flames.

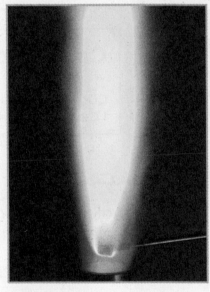

Compounds that contain sodium (such as salt = sodium chloride) have bright yellow flames.

✔ Quick Check

41. One way you can tell water from carbon dioxide is _____

_____.

42. Heating a compound may help you tell what is in it because _____

_____.

How are compounds used?

People today are finding many uses for compounds. For example, crude oil is a mixture of many useful products. It can be separated into gasoline, kerosene, diesel fuel, heating oil, and light fuel gases. These products are hydrocarbons (high•druh•KAHR•buhns). **Hydrocarbons** are compounds of hydrogen and carbon.

We use hydrocarbons every day. We use gasoline to run cars. We use oil and natural gas for heating. Rubber is made of hydrocarbons. We use rubber in tires, erasers, and the wrap on electrical wires.

Plastics are compounds made of long strings of carbon with other elements. Plastics are used to make paints, furniture, boats, and toys.

Clothing is made of natural compounds of cotton and wool, as well as of human-made compounds like polyester or nylon.

✔ Quick Check

43. Why are compounds important to us? _____

_____

LOG ON **e-Review** Summaries and quizzes online @ **www.macmillanmh.com**

Types of Matter

density	element	mass	mixture	matter	metal
metalloid	molecule	nonmetal	solution	volume	

Fill in the blanks with a word from the box.

1. _____ the space an object takes up

2. _____ the amount of matter in an object

3. _____ anything that has mass and volume

4. _____ a measure of how tightly matter is packed

5. _____ the simplest kind of substance there is

6. _____ a particle that contains more than one atom joined together

7. _____ a substance that conducts heat and electricity well

8. _____ a combination of substances that keep their properties

9. _____ an element that is a poor conductor

10. _____ one of a group of elements that have properties of metals and nonmetals

11. _____ a mixture that stays mixed

Fill in each blank with a letter to spell out the answer.

1. the smallest particle of an element __ __ __ __
   ₅

2. a mixture in which the particles settle and separate over time

   __ __ __ __ __ __ __ __ __ __
       1   4

3. the part of a solution that does the dissolving __ __ __ __ __ __ __ __
                  2   9

4. the part of a solution that gets dissolved __ __ __ __ __ __
             13

5. a way of separating particles of different sizes

   __ __ __ __ __ __ __ __ __
   12   3

6. a change in matter that produces a new substance with new

   properties __ __ __ __ __ __ __ __
           7 8

7. a substance formed when two or more other substances are

   combined and a chemical change takes place __ __ __ __ __ __ __
                  6

8. compounds made of hydrogen and carbon

   __ __ __ __ __ __ __ __ __ __ __
          10   11

Use the letters in the numbered blanks to answer the riddle.

Riddle: What is the name of the list of the building blocks all matter is made of? (**Clue:** The name is two words.)

__ __ __ __ __ __ __ __   __ __ __ __ __
1 2 3 4 5 6 7 8   9 10 11 12 13

CHAPTER 8

Changes in Matter

Vocabulary

chemical reaction a change in which substances before the change are different from those after the change

reactant a substance before a chemical reaction happens

product a substance that is formed by a chemical reaction

reactive how easily a substance takes part in a chemical reaction

metal a substance that lets heat and electricity pass through easily

conductor anything that lets heat and electricity flow through easily

insulator something that prevents heat, electricity, and even sound from moving through

alloy a mixture of two or more metals and nonmetals

How does one substance become another?

salt a compound made of a metal and a nonmetal

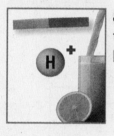

acid a substance that tastes sour and can be biting

indicator something that changes color in ways that let you identify a substance

base a substance that tastes bitter and turns litmus paper blue

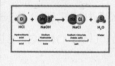

neutralize to add an acid and base together so that each cancels out the effects of the other

pH scale a measure of the strength of an acid or a base

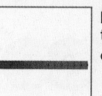

What are chemical changes?

Matter is going through *chemical changes* all around you. That is, substances are changing into other substances. Bread bakes. Iron rusts. Wood burns. Milk gets sour.

A chemical change in which you start with one substance (or more) and end up with a new substance (or more) is a **chemical reaction** (ree•AK•shuhn). The substances before the change are the **reactants** (ree•AK•tuhnts). The **products** are the new substances after the change.

What happens in a chemical reaction? The atoms and molecules in the reactants are rearranged. The rearranged particles form the products.

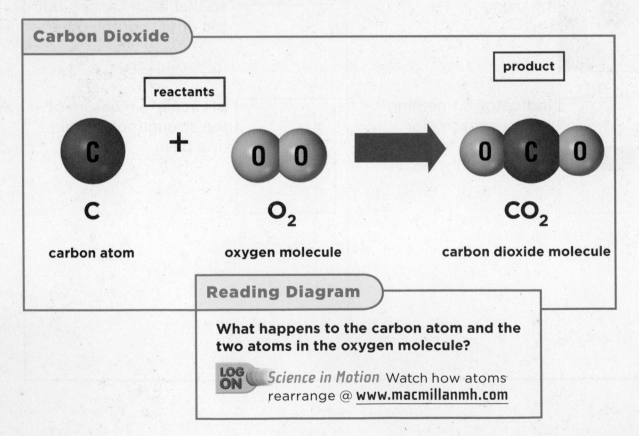

Carbon Dioxide

product

reactants

C + O O → O C O

C   O₂   CO₂

carbon atom   oxygen molecule   carbon dioxide molecule

Reading Diagram

What happens to the carbon atom and the two atoms in the oxygen molecule?

LOG ON *Science in Motion* Watch how atoms rearrange @ **www.macmillanmh.com**

This diagram shows a simple way to make carbon dioxide. Vinegar is added to baking soda. The products are water, bubbles of carbon dioxide, and a white powder (sodium acetate). See how the atoms rearrange themselves. There are just as many atoms of each kind before and after the reaction. So the total mass of the reactants equals the total mass of the products.

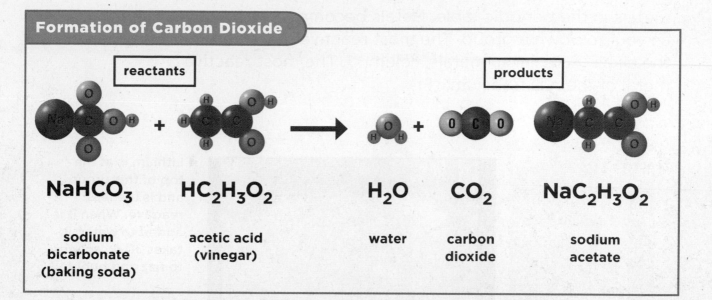

Formation of Carbon Dioxide

reactants

products

$NaHCO_3$

sodium bicarbonate (baking soda)

$HC_2H_3O_2$

acetic acid (vinegar)

H_2O

water

CO_2

carbon dioxide

$NaC_2H_3O_2$

sodium acetate

Here are two reactions in nature. In photosynthesis, green plants use sunlight and two reactants to produce food (a sugar).

water + carbon dioxide ⟶ sugar + oxygen

Plants and animals (and other living things) use that sugar to get energy in a chemical reaction called respiration.

sugar + oxygen ⟶ water + carbon dioxide

✓ Quick Check

1. How are these last two chemical reactions alike? Different?

_____

_____

Which elements are most likely to change?

An iron fence is likely to rust unless you protect it. Iron is more reactive (ree•AK•tiv) than many other elements. **Reactive** means how easily a substance takes part in a chemical reaction.

To tell how reactive a metal is, look at any column of metals in the periodic table. Metals become *more* reactive as you go *down* a group. The most reactive metals are the alkali (AL•kuh•ligh) metals, column 1. The most reactive metal of them is francium, (Fr).

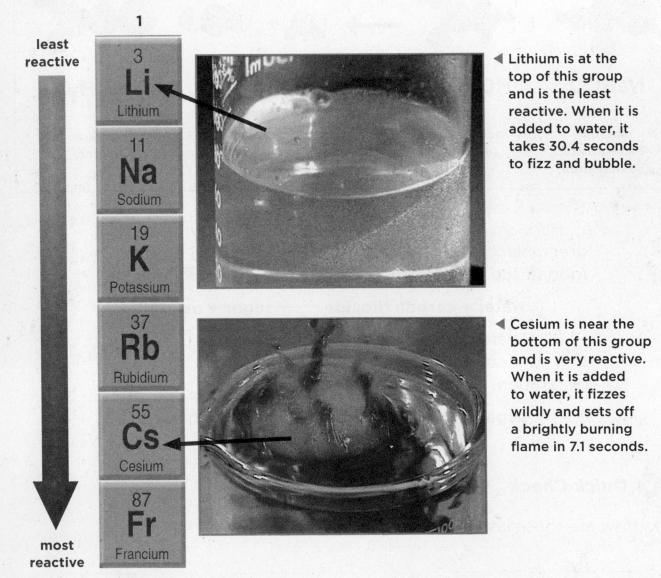

least reactive

1

| 3 |
| **Li** |
| Lithium |

| 11 |
| **Na** |
| Sodium |

| 19 |
| **K** |
| Potassium |

| 37 |
| **Rb** |
| Rubidium |

| 55 |
| **Cs** |
| Cesium |

| 87 |
| **Fr** |
| Francium |

most reactive

▲ The alkali metals

◀ Lithium is at the top of this group and is the least reactive. When it is added to water, it takes 30.4 seconds to fizz and bubble.

◀ Cesium is near the bottom of this group and is very reactive. When it is added to water, it fizzes wildly and sets off a brightly burning flame in 7.1 seconds.

Nonmetals

Nonmetals are reactive in an opposite way. Find any column of the periodic table that has nonmetals. The most reactive nonmetal is at the top of the column. Nonmetals become *less* reactive as you go *down* a column.

For example, oxygen is at the top of column 16. It is a reactive gas that combines with many metals.

The most reactive nonmetals are in column 17, the halogens. The most reactive of them are the two gases at the top, fluorine (Fl) and chlorine (Cl). For example, when chlorine combines with the metal sodium, the two elements disappear in a flash of light. They have formed table salt.

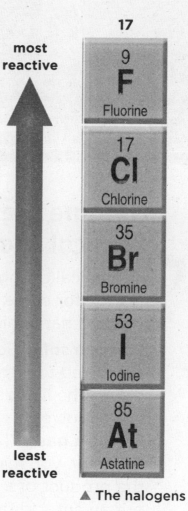

▲ The halogens

✔ Quick Check

Write *more* or *less* in each blank.

2. Potassium is _____ reactive than lithium.

3. Fluorine is _____ reactive than bromine.

4. Metals are _____ reactive as you go up a group.

5. Nonmetals are _____ reactive as you go up a group.

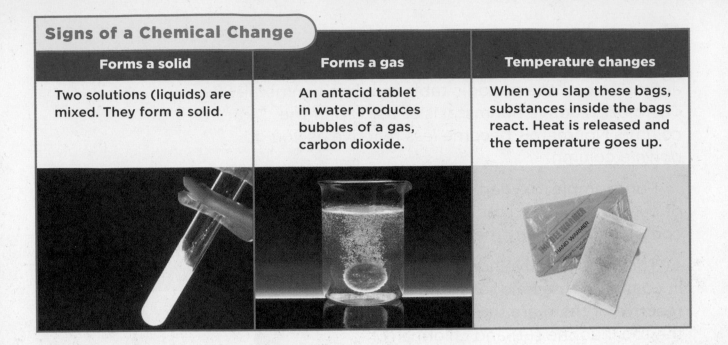

Signs of a Chemical Change

Forms a solid	Forms a gas	Temperature changes
Two solutions (liquids) are mixed. They form a solid.	An antacid tablet in water produces bubbles of a gas, carbon dioxide.	When you slap these bags, substances inside the bags react. Heat is released and the temperature goes up.

What are the signs of a chemical change?

Chemical changes are going on all around. You can look for some signs that tell you a chemical change is happening.

- **Forms a solid** Sometimes when two solutions are mixed together, a chemical reaction takes place. The liquids form a solid. The solid does not dissolve.

- **Forms a gas** When two substances are mixed together, you might see bubbles of gas. The gas is the product of a chemical reaction. For example, put an antacid tablet into water. The reaction on page 181 takes place and bubbles of carbon dioxide are produced.

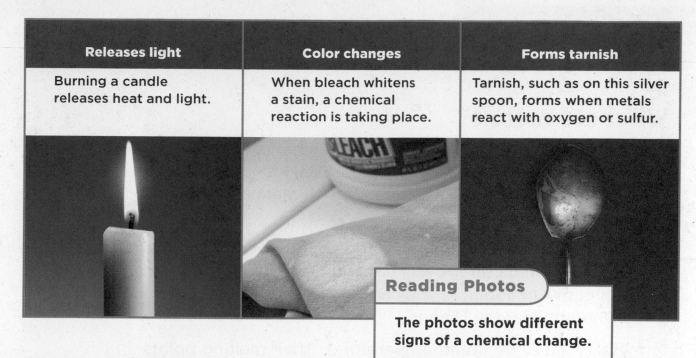

Releases light	Color changes	Forms tarnish
Burning a candle releases heat and light.	When bleach whitens a stain, a chemical reaction is taking place.	Tarnish, such as on this silver spoon, forms when metals react with oxygen or sulfur.

Reading Photos

The photos show different signs of a chemical change.

Energy and Color

- **Releases energy** You may see or feel energy given off in a chemical reaction. The energy may be heat, light, or both. For example, burning wood releases heat and light.
- **Color changes** If bleach is poured on a stain, the stain turns white.

If a drop of reddish iodine is put on a potato, the red turns black. These color changes indicate a chemical change.

- **Forms tarnish** Metals may turn rusty, black, or green when they react with oxygen or sulfur. The changed color is tarnish.

✔ *Quick Check*

Fill in three facts to explain the summary.

6. _____

_____

_____

7. _____

_____

8. _____

_____

Summary: You can look for signs of a chemical change.

LOG ON **e-Review** Summaries and quizzes online @ www.macmillanmh.com

What are metals?

About three-fourths (75%) of all the elements are metals. Copper (Cu), silver (Ag), iron (Fe), aluminum (Al), zinc (Zn), and lead (Pb) are some common metals. What are metals like?

A **metal** is substance that is a good conductor of heat and electricity. A **conductor** allows heat and electricity to flow through easily. In addition, you can often tell metals by their shine when they are polished.

Metals melt at different temperatures. Their melting points make some metals very useful. For example, mercury melts at a very low temperature, –39°C (–38.2°F). So, mercury is a liquid at room temperature. Mercury is used in one kind of barometer. It is the silvery liquid that rises or falls when air pressure changes.

Copper (Cu) nuggets like these may be the earliest metals used by humans.

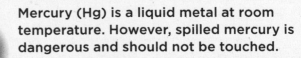

Mercury (Hg) is a liquid metal at room temperature. However, spilled mercury is dangerous and should not be touched.

Useful Melting Points

When mercury is warmed, it expands evenly. When it cools, mercury shrinks (contracts) evenly. Because of this property, mercury is used in most thermometers to show temperature changes.

However, the metal gallium (Ga) melts at 30°C (86°F). It stays a liquid up to a very high temperature. It boils at 2403°C (4357°F). So gallium is used in thermometers that measure high temperatures.

Metals with very high melting points are useful because they stay solid at high temperatures. Titanium has a melting point of 1668°C (3034°F). It is also strong and lightweight. So it is used to make aircraft and spacecraft. Beryllium, with an almost as high melting point, is used for wheel brakes of the space shuttle.

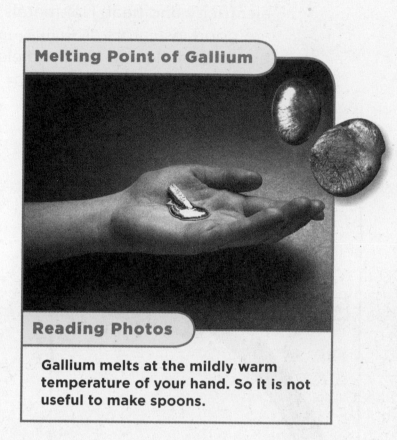

Melting Point of Gallium

Reading Photos

Gallium melts at the mildly warm temperature of your hand. So it is not useful to make spoons.

✔ Quick Check

Match the metal with the description.

9. ____ gallium   **a.** used in barometers and thermometers

10. ____ mercury   **b.** used to make spacecraft

11. ____ titanium   **c.** melts in your hand

12. What do metals have in common? _____

_____

What do metals have in common?

Remember, metals are good conductors of electricity and heat. Nonmetals, on the other hand, are good insulators (IN•suh•lay•tuhrs). An **insulator** helps prevent the flow of heat and electricity. Wood and plastic are insulators.

- **Conducting electricity** Metals such as copper and aluminum are used to make electrical wires. These metals conduct electricity from power plants to towns and inside your home.

- **Conducting heat** Pots and pans are usually made of metals so that the heat can spread evenly through the cookware and into the food inside them. Handles and gloves are made of insulators such as wood or plastic. Car engines are made of metals. The metal conducts heat away so that the engines do not overheat.

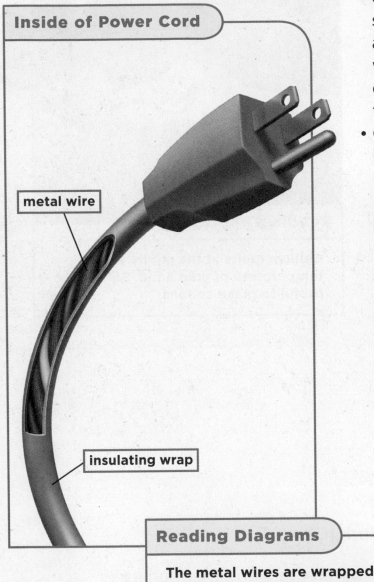

Inside of Power Cord

metal wire

insulating wrap

Reading Diagrams

The metal wires are wrapped with an insulator (plastic or rubber). The insulator prevents electric shock if the cord is touched.

▲ The metal sodium (Na) is soft enough to cut with a knife. It is very reactive, so gloves are used when holding it.

How hard are metals?

Glass and wood can break if you try to bend them. However, you can bend metal rods without breaking them. Many metals can be rolled or pounded into flat sheets without shattering. Gold can be pounded into thin sheets.

Some metals stretch into strands of wire when they are pulled. Copper and aluminum, for example, are made into wires. They can also be rolled like dough into sheets.

You may think iron is very hard. However, most metals can be dented. The deeper a dent is, the softer the metal. Chromium (Cr) is the hardest metal. Cesium (Cs) is the softest.

Pure copper, silver, and gold are soft. Jewelry made from these metals is often mixed with other metals to make a hard mixture of metals. The mixture does not scratch as easily as the pure metal.

✔ **Quick Check**

13. Circle the row that has three properties of metals:

used as insulators	breaks	snaps
used as conductors	drawn into wires	pounded flat
used as conductors	cracks when pulled	splinters

What are metal compounds?

What happens when iron rusts? Atoms of iron combine with atoms of a nonmetal, oxygen. The product, rust, is a compound—iron oxide.

When silver tarnishes, silver atoms combine with atoms of sulfur. The product, tarnish, is a compound called silver sulfide. When copper atoms combine with oxygen, tarnish is also formed—the compound copper oxide.

Rust and tarnish gradually "eat away" a metal. They weaken the metal so that it crumbles.

Reactive metals are the quickest to be "eaten away." The metal sodium reacts with oxygen so fast that they must be stored in oil to keep air out. In some cases, the compound that forms (such as aluminum oxide) coats the metal. The coating protects the metal.

Rust has turned a useful machine into a crumbling piece of junk.

✔ Quick Check

14. What is rust? _____

_____

15. Why do metals need to be protected against rust and tarnish?

_____

_____

What are alloys?

People can improve the usefulness of some metals melting them and mixing other elements with them. The products, when cooled and harden, are solid mixtures called alloys (AL•oyz). An **alloy** is a mixture of two or more metals and nonmetals.

For example, mixing gold with copper, silver, or other metals can make it stronger. Iron is soft and weak until carbon and metals such as chromium and nickel are added to make a hard alloy, steel. These two metals also protect the steel from being "eaten away."

Brass is an alloy made of copper and zinc. Musical instruments made from brass, such as trumpets, have a bright sound quality. Bronze, a long lasting alloy, is made of copper and tin.

Medical tools are made of an alloy of tungsten. This alloy allows the tools to be razor sharp.

People who lived in the Bronze Age knew how make bronze. They used this alloy to make strong tools and weapons.

✔ Quick Check

In each row, cross out a word that does not belong.

16. bronze   oxygen   copper   tin

17. sulfur   brass   copper   zinc

18. steel   iron   chlorine   chromium

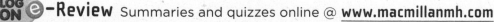

LOG ON **e-Review** Summaries and quizzes online @ **www.macmillanmh.com**

What is a salt?

You sprinkle it on food. It looks like little grains. What is it? It's table salt. There are actually many kinds of salt. Table salt is just one kind of salt. It is a compound called sodium chloride.

A **salt** is any compound made of a metal and a nonmetal. In sodium chloride, sodium is the metal and chlorine is the nonmetal.

The particles that make up salt are lined up in orderly rows. This orderly arrangement gives salts a boxlike shape and makes them hard. It's hard to melt salts. They have high melting points. Table salt melts at 801°C (1,474°F)!

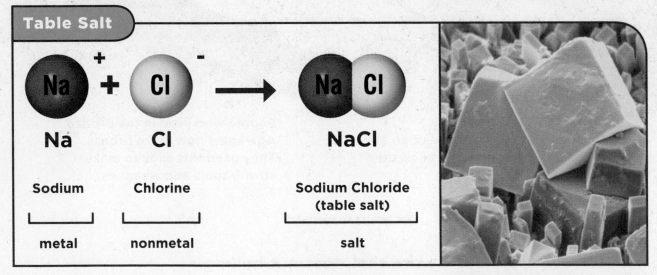

Table Salt

Na	+	Cl	→	Na Cl
Na		Cl		NaCl
Sodium		Chlorine		Sodium Chloride (table salt)
metal		nonmetal		salt

▲ Table salt is made of a metal (Na) and a nonmetal (Cl). Up close, you can see its boxlike salt grains.

Making Salts

One way to make salts is to mix two compounds called an acid (A•sed) and a base. See that the acid in the diagram has chlorine (Cl) in it. The base has sodium (Na). When the two compounds react, the Na and Cl join to became NaCl (salt).

When salts are dissolved in water the metal particles and nonmetal particles break apart. They have electric charges (+ and –):

$$NaCl \text{ (in water)} \longrightarrow Na^+ + Cl^-$$

These charged particles carry electricity through water. So a mixture of salt and water can be a good conductor. However, some salts do not dissolve well in water. They do not make good conductors when added to water.

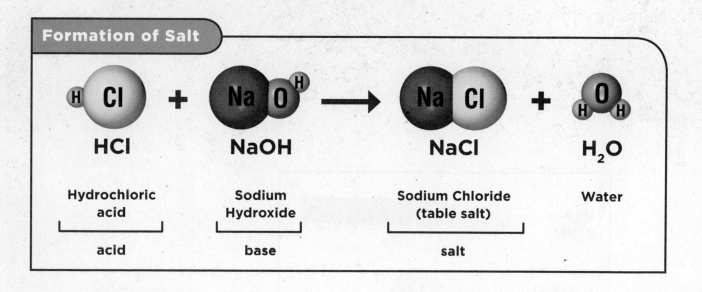

Formation of Salt

HCl	NaOH	NaCl	H₂O
Hydrochloric acid	Sodium Hydroxide	Sodium Chloride (table salt)	Water
acid	base	salt	

✔ Quick Check

Cross out the item that does not belong in each row.

19. metal   Na   Cl   sodium

20. nonmetal   Na   Cl   chlorine

21. To make a good conductor, a salt must _____

_____

What are acids and bases?

An orange tastes sour. Squeeze a drop of orange juice on litmus (LIT•muhs) paper. Lemon juice makes the paper turn red.

Litmus paper is an indicator (IN•duh•kay•duhr). An **indicator** changes color in ways to help you tell what a substance is. The red color indicates that orange juice is an acid. An **acid** is a substance that tastes sour and turns blue litmus paper red. **Be careful:** Never taste unfamiliar substances to tell if they are acids.

Other acids are lemon juice and vinegar. The formula for any acid starts with **H** (hydrogen). For example, hydrochloric acid is **H**Cl. When you mix an acid and water, hydrogen particles are formed. The hydrogen particles have an electric charge. They conduct electricity through water.

$$\text{acid + water} \longrightarrow \text{H}^+$$

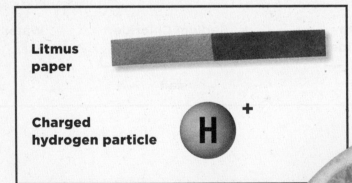

Litmus paper

Charged hydrogen particle

Citrus fruits (such as oranges and lemons) contain an acid. ▶

Bases

Soap and ammonia cleaner contain bases. A **base** is a substance that tastes bitter and turns red litmus paper blue. Bases feel slippery, like soap. **Be careful:** Never taste or feel unfamiliar substances to tell if they are bases.

The formula for a base ends in **OH** (oygen + hydrogen). When a base is added to water, a charged particle is formed from the **OH**. These charged particles carry electricity in water.

$$\text{base} + \text{water} \longrightarrow \text{OH}^-$$

When an acid is mixed with a base, they form a salt. The acid supplies the nonmetal part of the salt. The base supplies the metal part.

Acids and bases neutralize (NEW•truh•lyze) each other. **Neutralize** means "to cancel each other out." That is, the salt that is produced is not an acid or a base.

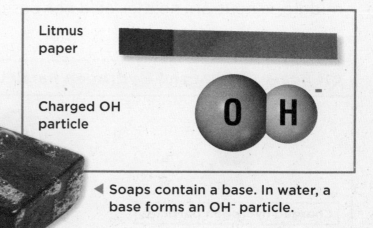

Litmus paper

Charged OH particle

◀ Soaps contain a base. In water, a base forms an OH⁻ particle.

✔ Quick Check

Fill in the diagram. How are acids and bases alike? Different?

Acids (different)   Alike   Bases (different)

22. _____   **23.** Both are tested with   **24.** _____

_____   _____   _____

_____   _____   _____

How strong are acids and bases?

Some acids are stronger than others. For example, a strong acid can wear away a hole in metal quickly. Vinegar on the other hand is a weak acid. It's weak enough for you to use on a salad with no effect.

Some bases are stronger than others. For example, lye is a strong base in drain cleaners. It can "eat away" a clog in a drain quickly.

The strength of acids and bases is measured on a **pH scale**. The scale runs from 0 (strong acid, weak base) to 14 (strong base, weak acid). A rating of 7, right in the middle, is neutral—neither acid nor base.

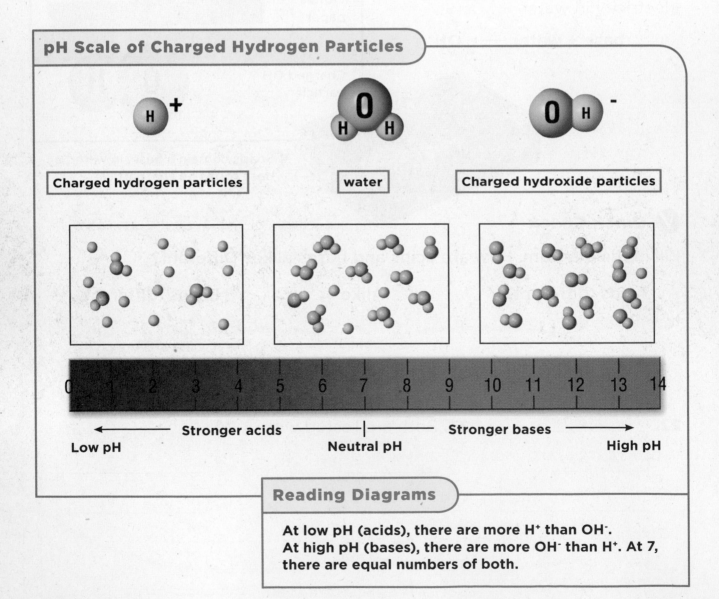

pH Scale of Charged Hydrogen Particles

Charged hydrogen particles | water | Charged hydroxide particles

0 1 2 3 4 5 6 7 8 9 10 11 12 13 14

← Stronger acids ——— | ——— Stronger bases →

Low pH | Neutral pH | High pH

Reading Diagrams

At low pH (acids), there are more H$^+$ than OH$^-$.
At high pH (bases), there are more OH$^-$ than H$^+$. At 7, there are equal numbers of both.

Reading the pH Scale

Strong acids form many charged hydrogen particles (**H⁺**) when added to water. They have very few **OH⁻** particles. For example, an acid with a pH of 0 or 1 forms many more **H⁺** than an acid with a pH of 5 or 6.

Strong bases have very few **H⁺** particles in water. They form, instead, many **OH⁻** particles. Bases with a pH of 13 or 14 have many more **OH⁻** particles than a base with a pH of 8 or 9.

Water has a pH of 7. It has about the same number of **H⁺** and **OH⁻** particles. Water is neutral. That is, it is neither an acid nor a base.

Scientists use meters to measuring the pH of water and soil. A pH near 0 (very acid) can be very harmful for living things in a lake or river. Most plants grow best when the soil has a pH over 7 (base) rather than under (acid).

Hydrangeas have blue flowers when grown in soil that has a pH under 7 (acid). They have pink flowers when the pH of the soil is above 7 (base). ▶

✓ Quick Check

Write *acid* or *base* next to each description.

25. pH under 7 _____

26. More **H⁺** particles than **OH⁻** particles _____

27. pH over 7 _____

How do we use salts?

Salt was used as money in some ancient cultures. Why was it so valuable? In days when there were no freezers, salt kept foods from spoiling. Salts remove water from foods. Bacteria cannot survive in foods dried with salt. Fish has been packed in salt in many places for centuries.

Salt is used for seasoning. Small amounts of salt along with other flavorings give many meals a rich flavor. Salt is also used for curing meats and baking. It is used for canning foods and pickling foods.

Salt is also very useful in icy weather. If you spread salt onto ice, it dissolves into the ice and lowers the freezing point. The ice turns to slush or water and is easy to remove.

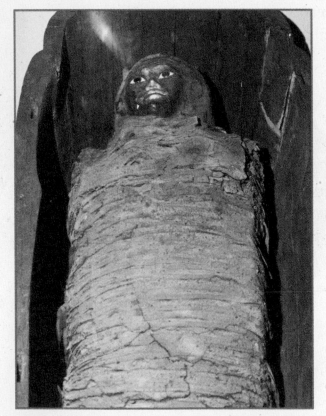

Mummies were dried in salt by ancient people of Egypt. A number of them have remained preserved for over 2,000 years.

Salt spreaders are hard at work to ease the removal of snow and ice from the road.

Where is salt found?

Combining an acid and a base makes a salt. However, to meet our need for salt, we collect salt that is already made in nature.

Salt was formed early in Earth's history. It was dissolved by rain and ended up in the oceans. Today, there are as much as 3.5 kg (7.7 lb) of salt in every 100 kg (220 lb) of ocean water.

In many places today, ocean water is drawn into shallow pools. Exposed to the Sun, the water evaporates. The salt remains behind.

Early in Earth's history, salt remained behind when shallow inland seas dried up. Over time the salt was buried by sediments. We can get this salt by pumping water down into the salt. The water becomes salty. We collect the water and let it evaporate. The salt remains behind.

These sea side pools are used for getting salt.

✅ Quick Check

Write *true* or *false* for each sentence. Correct any false statement.

28. Salt evaporates from ocean water. _____

29. Salt raises the freezing point of water. _____

30. Salt can preserve foods. _____

LOG ON **e-Review** Summaries and quizzes online @ www.macmillanmh.com

Changes in Matter

Choose the letter of the best answer.

1. Anything that lets heat and electricity flow through easily is a(n)

   a. compound

   b. insulator

   c. reactant

   d. conductor

2. A change in which substances before the change are different from those after the change is called a(n)

   a. reactant

   b. physical change

   c. chemical reaction

   d. indicator

3. When an acid is added to a base, the two substances can

   a. form an acid

   b. form a base

   c. become more reactive

   d. neutralize each other

4. A measure of the strength of an acid or a base is the

   a. chemical change

   b. pH scale

   c. salt content

   d. metal content

5. A substance before a chemical reaction happens is called a(n)

   a. reactant   c. metal

   b. salt   d. product

6. A substance that is formed by a chemical reaction is a(n)

   a. product   c. insulator

   b. conductor   d. indicator

7. Something that prevents heat, electricity, and even sound from moving through is a(n)

   a. acid

   b. conductor

   c. reactant

   d. insulator

Read each clue. Write the answers in the blanks to fill in the crossword puzzle.

Across

2. a compound made of a metal and a nonmetal

3. a mixture of two or more metals and nonmetals

5. something that changes color in ways that let you identify a substance

Down

1. a substance that lets heat and electricity pass through easily

3. a substance that tastes sour and can be biting

4. a substance that tastes bitter and turns litmus paper blue

6. how easily a substance takes part in a chemical reaction

Credits